# Teach Like a Diamond

# Teach Like A Diamond

*Dynamic Teaching for New Teachers*

*By*

DIAMOND EMERALD

ISBN: 978-1-7378224-0-0 (Paperback)

Front Cover design/artist/Image:
Sophisticated Press LLC & VaLarie Humphrey

Printed in the United States of America

**Published By Diamond Emerald**

Publishing Consultant

SOPHISTICATED
P R E S S

# ACKNOWLEDGMENTS

This is dedicated to Diamond Hudson & Madeline Emelda Skinner. The OG Diamond & Emerald. This is dedicated to every Teacher who thought they weren't good enough and would not survive. This is for every Teacher who knows they're good enough but is struggling to find their way. The pressure will create the Dynamic Diamond Teacher that is You.

Romans 8:28

# Table of Contents

# CHAPTER 1

# S - Show Up & Smile

*"Go home Diamond"*

Those were the words spoken to me by my principal on March 13th, 2020. A day that will live in educational infamy.

Yet I had memories of early February. The COVID.19 Pandemic had begun to slowly but persistently invade our peculiar island of Manhattan. I remember how the days on the subways began changing. Masks were being worn by more than the random health-conscious elderly person. I knew things had started to shift when a beautiful black millennial woman strutted on the train with shiny black boots, skinny jeans, box braids, faux eyeglasses ( just for style ) - and a face mask. I went to work and asked my fellow Teachers, "Are we doing this now?"

Little did I know - how could anyone have known - that those were the last days.

### The "S" in "Shine Brite" stands for "Show Up & Smile".

*Don't Smile until November* is not a rule for today's teacher. I do not mean to offend you. That is not my intention, dear teacher. We are in a new era, so lend me your ears! The mighty warriors of the education system have experienced a shift as monumental as the Transcontinental Drift and I have come to shed light on the situation.

We have transitioned to hybrid learning. Hybrid refers to the nature of learning that exists as a result of the COVID-19 Pandemic and the closing of school buildings. Hybrid refers to the fact that students could be engaged in learning via a computer or in person or both. Some school systems are "all remote" or "all virtual" which means all students receive instruction online all the time. Some school systems are "in-person" which means all students still attend school in person and the teachers provide in-person instruction. There may be smaller class sizes, alternative bell schedules, or at the minimum mask-wearing. Some school systems are "blended" or "hybrid" which means they engage in a mix of the two systems. I am calling education systems that exist during and post 2020 "hybrid learning". This includes in-person instruction with masks and social distancing. We must integrate (or at minimum address) technology and the time school buildings were closed in today's education environment. Therefore, we are all hybrid educators!

Some school systems have teachers entering the building and teaching kids remotely; this is hybrid teaching. If students come into the building and learn from computers as teachers stream lessons, this is hybrid teaching. When teachers enter the building and teach some kids online and some kids in the building; this is hybrid teaching. When kids enter the building and use computers for some activities but not all, this is hybrid teaching.

Does that last one sound familiar? It should. Nothing is new under the sun, beloved teacher. If you were in the game before this, you have greatness stored in you. If you are new to this game, greatness is waiting to be unleashed in you. It starts with "Showing Up and Smiling".

## Show Up

"Showing Up," like any wonderful diamond, is multifaceted. One must physically wake up every day and decide to continue on this march. Much of our current existence is completely out of our control. When public schools closed on March 13th in New York City the multitude of this teaching force had to make the decision to *show up* the next day and not call in sick. Without being properly prepared, teachers managed to get themselves online to Google Meets and Google Classroom platforms. They posted work and adapted pre-made virtual lessons. They tapped into old accounts and posted lessons from online sources. They swapped passwords and resources like snacks during lunch. We did that!

What made my school's transition so successful was the ability to pre-plan. We spent the two in-school days before the school closure announcement having teachers plan the transition to remote learning. Therefore when the Department Of Education (DOE) gave us two days to plan the following week, my school was prepared to check and assess systems. Part of Showing Up means knowing what you are showing up for. School buildings are a hub of news. It is your job as a teacher to discern amongst the noise. It is the job of the school leaders to attune their ears to multiple voices (or social media platforms) to have any sense of reality. We were two days ahead. It did not make the situation any less real. But at least all of our kids had Google accounts.

I heard horror story after horror story about how difficult it was for school systems that had no online presence for their students; they had to turn it around. Administrators, teachers, and paraprofessionals had to create email accounts for students using platforms they were not familiar with.

Art and science teachers were begging to return to their buildings to retrieve the physical artifacts that bring their subjects to life. All of us, from the STEAM teacher to the Speech provider, had to show up in new ways. Yet on Monday March 16th, the first day of all remote instruction (which ended up being a professional development day for most ) all teachers still had to Show Up. Not knowing what the day or our profession looked like, we showed up. Day after day of shifting winds. This means our mental, social, physical, and spiritual center needs to be solid. This meant Showing Up in advance when you could.

Being a morning person is essential for being a teacher. Getting ahead on the day is what can prevent the inevitable mishaps of daily teaching. Co-planning times must be sacred. Check-ins from admin or and fellow teachers and teacher leaders ensure cohesion and overall well-being. We had to physically show up for our students who were feeling lost and needed us as the touchpoint. Magic was happening in the building and I know so many of us were on the brink of a breakthrough with some of our students. What could we do now? Show Up! And we must keep finding ways to Show Up in our student's lives.

The first online unit I conducted included asynchronous work (work that is assigned online but does not include live instruction from an educator) focussed on a Women's History Project. I Showed Up for my students by ensuring they still had ways to see my face and hear my voice. We were very unsure of students' abilities to get online. So if they missed our live class they had documents with embedded hyperlinks to me explaining the task. I could use resources like Screencast-O-Matic to read through directions and answer questions I thought they posed. I recorded myself reading an entire novel because I knew my students would not only enjoy my reading but my students required it to obtain the content knowledge. In-person- I would have read aloud. Now, I spent the morning hours reading and recording <u>Mauz</u> while examining the landscape outside my fire escape. I Showed Up.

And if I had not, my students would have suffered. Which means their families would have suffered. Which means their neighborhoods would have suffered. Which means their city would have suffered. Which means their state would have suffered. Which means their region would have suffered. Which means our country would have suffered.

I am very clear on how essential it is to have dynamic, diamond-quality instruction. Instruction that demonstrates the pressure that comes from teaching and the joy and brilliance that comes out of it. Teaching that is tested by the cuts we get and illuminated by the student progress made.

Now I am at the point where I can create a complete virtual Bitmoji classroom with links to both content-based engagement and Social-Emotional Learning (SEL). But my Showing Up has shifted to focus more on the live teaching experience. We were creating e-learning policies as we implemented them. We had to show up for each other and teach one another how to set up these meetings and how to track attendance. Admin and support staff showed up by scheduling and identifying the correct platforms to use right away. Once those platforms were up and running, we began to post work and set up live meetings.

Those of us who have been doing this (leading live meetings) know the anxiety that comes from commencing an e-meeting. The time between posting a link, opening the room, and students logging on can be a stress that causes your heart to beat out of your chest!

*"Did I post it to the right students? Will they see it in time? Are they using the correct email? Will someone else get this link? Will my Wi-Fi go out? Will the Wi-Fi of my target students go out? What if they don't show up? My schedule has changed, do I actually have these students*

*now? What if my baby wakes and I am five minutes late to class? Will students abandon class and leave?"*

After going through all of that mentally, suddenly you hear the *ping* sound or you see students requesting to join your Google Meet! Before you push that *admit* button, take a breath (not a deep one, we do not have time for that!) and brighten your face.

## The pandemic was traumatizing. Smiles are healing.

Due to the induced trauma of the pandemic, smiles can and will be an essential connector between screens for teachers and their students. Some of us will, and have, met our students from a virtual perceptive only. It is essential to be on camera and to smile while doing it. A smile provides comfort and ensures we are not asking anything of them, that we are not modeling ourselves. Maybe you do not feel like physically smiling, or that is just not your personality type. Your environment should smile! You can create Bitmojis, ARemojois, and other apps to create a cartoon or virtual avatar for your teacher persona. Allow the cartoon to be the silly welcoming visage for your classroom.

As a way to welcome incoming 5th-grade applicants in the midst of the pandemic, we were instructed to create our Bitmojis to add to the group picture that would be displayed in the hallway. This replaced what used to be our physical pictures displayed on the welcoming bulletin board. The message we were sending was *This is what we do now. This is what we look like virtually.* And guess what? We still love what we do and will do our best to teach and love you. We have created a Smile to introduce our kids to our community.

How do you Smile during every lesson? It should come right at the beginning. This could be in the form of a fun intro game/video to ease students into the lesson. One of my classes, more than the others, includes some latecomers. This class includes a wide range of learners but is a class of fewer than ten students. I was struggling with the feeling I had to wait until I had a full class to teach the meat of the content. I began to implement a picture game video from YouTube. The video displays close-ups of images and slowly pans out to reveal the full image. Viewers have about twenty-five seconds to guess what the image is. I learned this at a free Professional Development (PD). I play the video for no more than three minutes and I love to hear kids yell out their guesses or write in the chat. Sometimes it is the only time I hear some of the most struggling student's voices during the lesson. It is not ideal, but I will take the engagement!

That is what giving access looks like. This is still an intellectual activity and I can gather data on a student's ability to understand or estimate spatial relationships or cultural knowledge based on the groups of images. For instance, a recent week's video included food items. The blurry image zoomed out as it got into focus. One of my quieter students piped up to guess "Hennessy!" To their credit, the image was of a wine glass! But do you know how much knowledge I gained from their answer?! It is up to me to use that knowledge to benefit the child and strengthen our relationship. I could think negatively and follow the bias that this child may have 'negative alcoholic influences' in their lives. *Or* I could take joy in knowing this child has knowledge in food and drinks! And they have adults in their life that include them enough to know what they are drinking.

I am well aware of my students who have alcoholic parents. That was not that kind of trigger. My student took joy in being correct. The image was of a glass made for alcoholic drinks. I gave them the props! And if I wanted to, we could even keep daily track of points as a further incentive. This was their first win in my class that day! And even though their camera was not on, I could feel them smiling. Now they are set up for more wins in my class. Which sets me up to win as a teacher.

My Daily Gemstone Meditations are yet another way that I begin my classes with a Smile even when I physically cannot. I record and archive on YouTube daily messages for students called "Gemstones: Meditations & Motivation for Students". These videos feature a principle in Swahili to meditate on, and a song or message to be motivated by. While the video plays the children are instructed that they can turn off their cameras. When it concludes the video asks them to return. During this time teachers also can turn off their cameras or take attendance, or even take their bathroom break! So if you, dear teacher, are not physically able to smile, please borrow mine.

### Learning should promote joy!

Would students look at your space and smile? Are your slides engaging and clear? Does your outfit compliment your background? Are you encouraging? Are you funny? If not, use someone else's content! We are competing against expansive forces of engagement. I do not need to go down that road with you. So do not be stressed by the need to jazz up your e-look. Get excited about it! Or potentially lose your students due to your resistance.

Kirk Franklin's song *Smile* was an instant hit that described how imperative that physical facial gesture of a Smile is to the human experience. At the start of the school closures, I began remixing and creating covers of songs as I sought to reach out to our fellow teachers. Reference these lyrics or the song itself when you forget the tenets of this principle. My lyrics for the remix of *Smile* are:

> *"Today's a new day, but there is no sunshine*
> *Nothing but clouds, and it's dark in my heart*

*And it feels like a cold night*
*Today's a new day, but where are my Children!*

*Where is their love and their joy that they're promised*
*I told them it'd be alright*
*I almost gave up, but a power that I can't explain*
*Keeps me going so when the camera starts -*

*I smile, even though this hurts see I smile*
*I know my kids are working so I smile*
*We've been in quarantine a while*
*But I smile, smile*
*It's so hard to look up when we been down*
*I sure would hate to see you give up now*
*You look so much better when you smile, so smile*

*I almost gave up (last week) but a power that I can't explain*
*Keeps me going so when the camera starts*
*I smile, even though I hurt see I smile*
*I'm thankful Zoom is working so I smile!*
*Even though we're in it for a while*
*I smile, smile*

*It's so hard to look up when we been down*
*I sure would hate to see you give up now*
*You look so much better when you smile, so smile"*

**GEMs**

- ❖ Show Up for your students physically wherever they, or you are.

- ❖ Create a Smile with your environment by making your space inviting by adding a warm welcoming, music, and other artistic choices.

- ❖ Learning promotes joy! Create access points in your lessons where students can win!

# CHAPTER 2

# H - Humble Not Timid

Being a New Teacher is a cacophony of emotions, expectations, demands, trial and error, tears, binge eating, studying, not eating, and learning how to be a person. Far too many entities fail New Teachers in the area of *life*.

The title "New Teacher" has been reserved for an educator who has spent anywhere less than 5 years in the teaching field. Some people/institutions cut it off at 3 years. In New York City, this notion is intricately connected to tenure. Tenure is one of the privileges afforded to us who work in a system with a Union. It is a protection against unjust unemployment and a confirmation of your efficacy as an educator. During my time as an NYC teacher, the probationary period (I hate that term) lasted 2 years and you could apply for tenure during your third year working. Now they have pushed these guidelines back and teachers must wait an additional year and apply for tenure during their 3rd year of teaching, thereby having tenure as a 4th-year teacher. Once a teacher has tenure, nobody calls them new anymore.

But then, school buildings closed.

**The "H" in "Shine Brite" stands for "Humble and Not Timid".**

## <u>We are ALL New Teachers Now!</u>

I say this with boldness and excitement! But do not fret my vet! Embrace this new state we find ourselves in. There are genuinely great benefits to being a New Teacher. I have spent much of my adult life educating and supporting New Teachers. I have also had extensive experience being one. My school uses a rotating curriculum. Therefore, my second year at the school felt like another first year, since it was an entirely new flow and curriculum.

I have deep knowledge of being a New Teacher. I have served and supported hundreds of New Teachers through my work with NYC Teaching Fellows. Not only was I asked to return to coach New Teachers - I have also served in every role that can be held at a Training Academy Site. During the Spring and Summer months, NYC Teaching Fellows teach and learn in training academies across NYC. The purpose is to train New Teachers to engage in the school systems they will be working in. They are coached by a licensed teacher who shows them the ropes! Typically, in the spring, Fellows shadowed and taught lessons in NYC public school classrooms. In the summer, Fellows teach summer schools in various configurations around the city.

My time as an NYC Teaching Fellow was paramount to my life as a teacher. It was my pathway to teaching and I am forever grateful. In addition - it was incredibly fun! Let us further establish our New Teacher status.

➢ A New Teacher is: a Teacher who does not have experience teaching in the classroom. Similarly, most of us did not have experience teaching online.

➢ A New Teacher is: a Teacher who is unsure of their pay schedule and does not get paid for all the pre-work they must perform.

When the pandemic started there was a BIG question about if/and how our pay would be affected (including having vacation days or not). And some of us questioned if we would still have jobs the following year. Uncertainty about your salary is the life of a New Teacher.

➢ A New Teacher is: a Teacher who needs to learn how to develop relationships with kids since they have not established them yet. Hybrid teaching has created circumstances where teachers first meet kids virtually and never have the chance to connect in person. Even in the middle of the year in March, you may have become a new teacher again if you lost track of some kids and had to reestablish the connection.

➢ A New Teacher is: a Teacher who needs a great deal of guidance from the admin and is observed often. Many of us have desired far more input from our admin than ever before!

Lo and behold, we are ALL New Teachers! No one is teaching in the instructional setting they were hired in. I have listed some negative factors to get us all on the same page. However, there are many positives of being the babies of the field.

New Teachers are given grace. You know the New Teacher who wandered down the hall late to their class? Grace. You know the New Teacher who asked an awkward question in a whole staff meeting? Grace. You know the New Teacher who accidentally made way too many copies? Grace.

## Hybrid Teaching is Humbling.

If you want to shine like a Diamond you have to get cut like a Diamond. It is only through the mistakes I have made, and hurts I have lived through that I am able to produce this wisdom.

Everyone who was ever good at anything when it came to teaching had to switch it up, and up their game. Even the pros were panicking! One of the definite issues that would humble Ms. Frizzle herself is "The Camera Issue".

"The Camera Issue": Invariably, this issue has come up for every single online learning platform and for every teacher in the e-world. I have personally dealt with my feelings on this issue as an instructor of small children and adults. I have also been privy to a litany of conversations in various teacher forums about this topic. Some districts/school systems mandate student's cameras be on and some do not. Some districts/school systems have punitive practices for students who do not turn their cameras on. Some districts/school systems penalize teachers when students do not have their cameras on. Because of the mixed messaging, along with our personal biases, this is probably one of the most controversial teacher topics regarding hybrid teaching. Teachers have to fight this "The Camera Issue" daily. *Or do we?*

Educators understand the camera issue is an equity issue. My solution to this issue came from deep thought experiments and Socratic questioning of my peers, my students, and myself. On a basic level, do students have cameras on their devices? If they do, do they have the ability to hide their background? If a child is in the corner of a shelter and has no device with the green screen ability, why would they risk the public shame? Why do some kids always show their faces and some never do? If I did see their faces briefly, what was the antecedent for this? Why is this important to me? Am I engaging enough for kids to show their faces? Is my face pleasant? Is my camera angle and view pleasant? Why do I want their cameras on? Is it because I am gifted at identifying visual interaction? Or is it because I am not equipped enough to use other methods besides visible interaction? If we were in person how would I engage? Are there other ways that I can get students to engage? Is the child able to show an arm, hand, or top of the head for confirmation of activities? Is my desire based on content or connection? Are there other ways to demonstrate content or connection? What if the only thing they did was turn on their camera, is that sufficient?

*If I were a student in middle school right now would I be turning on my camera?*

My answer to my own last question was, *depends*. I was a great student, hardworking and compliant. Yet, my social standing and self-esteem were like a fragile fledgling in middle school. Nothing - absolutely nothing - would have gotten me to turn my camera on, at my all-white middle school, if my hair was not done. In the same manner, if there was a Youth Ministry Zoom call at my black church, and my hair was not done, I would not have turned my camera on. Jesus himself would have to intervene.

Hybrid teaching is now merging environments that before were separate. And we are doing this with little consistency. Which day is virtual and which day is in person? If the day is async (work is provided online with no live teaching) then students do not need a camera on. If we are in person some students need their hair done and their clothes ready. This constant fluctuation can be maddening. This does not include the various needs of the differently-abled students.

I know me. I know my kids. I know my teachers. We are not, and cannot be timid with our desires for our students to engage (regardless of their setting). We give clear "What to do Directions" (from Teach Like

A Champion), we restate the consequences for non-engagement, we call/message home when non-compliance exists. And, we stand tall and teach to black screens anyway! Being Humble and Not Timid leads me to one sound conclusion.

*There is NO direct correlation between Great Teaching and the number of student's cameras being on.*

If you were in their physical presence what would you be doing to engage them? How can you translate this online? Disengage with the camera harassment and focus on teaching content that is essential and promotes other types of engagement. Teachers have used the chat, private messages, Nearpod, Google Docs, Flipgrids, Google Slides, Desmos, Flocabulary Tasks, Peardecks, and Zoom Annotations to enable students to show comprehension of the material. And YOU are one of them!

Dear Teacher, it is NOT about YOU.

Or let me put it this way, *It's not you, it is everything else.* And their reasons for not wanting to put on their camera could simply be, *they do not want to.* And you have to be ok with that because it is out of your control. An administration that is encouraging you to harass students instead of engaging them is wrong. Detach your feelings about the issue. Then we can create release for ourselves and get back to teaching.

## GEMs

- ❖ Humility is not a part of just being a good New Teacher, it is a part of being a good person.

- ❖ Hybrid teaching is Humbling! Dynamic teaching is Not Timid!

- ❖ Embrace the positives of being a New Teacher again.

- ❖ Camera Issue? Let it Go!

# CHAPTER 3

# I - Inspire

Inspiration is the gift from the heavens to us lowly beings on earth. We are given insight to create beyond our limits and stretch ourselves to new heights. It is part of every teacher's job to inspire students on a daily basis. Why? Because freedom is not free. Intrinsic motivation is not inherently high amongst students. There is a direct correlation between the grade level and the lack of a love of learning. Middle school is that sweet spot in life where all the hope dies.

## The "I" in "Shine Brite" stands for "Inspire".

*"I loved middle school!"* is not a phrase one is likely to hear often. Even when the school experience is great- puberty tends to ruin everything. While I will not go into detail about everything that can go wrong - just take a moment to pause and reflect on your middle school experience. I must do this as a middle school teacher.

You must reflect on your stage in your life that matches the age of the students you serve. If you are a 4th grade teacher, go there. If you are a 12th grade teacher, go there. What were the needs/wants/concerns in your life? And what inspired you? You cannot reach out until you reach in. You cannot inspire someone that does not connect with you. Even if the inspiration comes from a negative situation, connection is still required! I am inspired by white supremacists to stop white supremacy. The message is clear and direct and passionate. I am inspired by Michelle Obama by her directive of *"when they go low we go high"*. Her message is clear, direct, passionate, and correct. Both stimuli move me to action. That is what we want from students, movement and action. I would rather a student complain to me that the assignment is "dumb" and propose a new idea, rather than not do it at all.

The heart of this inspiration is truly to get them to *want to do the work*. When students say that I am inspiring, they are saying *"I like the way she makes me feel"* and *"She makes me feel good about me"* and *"She makes me believe I can do things"*. That … is … it.

Now, if I design a task that they actually cannot accomplish, my inspiration is a lie. And I become a liar. Having confidence in my instruction is connected to having confidence in myself. In order to inspire my children, I have to be inspired. So, you should have reflected on what inspired you as a child in that grade. Did you find it? Was it good grades, money, rewards, a better life, music, church, sports, friends, celebrities, clothes, accomplishments, food, free time, love? Ok good. Now think about what is inspiring you now. Give it to your babies! Before I was able to identify what each child needed, I just gave them what worked for me.

## Music

Music has been a part of my teaching career since the very beginning. During my pre-service training experience with the New York City Teaching Fellows, I taught summer school in Queens. I and another pre-service teacher took turns teaching a group of fifteen 7th graders math and literacy. I could tell during my co-teacher's block of time that he completely lost the kids. I could feel the dead energy and I was not having it. I was being observed next. He was not about to kill my teaching career! I had talked to the students enough to have developed relationships with them. I had also seen the licensed teacher teach and knew how to imitate her command (let's go acting degrees!). I was also desperate enough to fail.

Therefore, during the five-minute transition period, I connected my phone to the speaker in the class. At that time I was using Pandora. I selected a specific popular hip-hop song that one of the more vocal girls had been singing. I announced we were having a stretch/dance break! I gave clear "What To Do" directions for the students to stand up and walk around the outside of the chairs. I encouraged them to dance and let out some energy. I played my girl's song and she immediately started to giggle and put her head down. I knew she wanted to twerk and I appreciated her restraint. She really was a beautiful girl, and she really had no idea. I walked next to her and danced. I also walked next to the quiet, shy, girl who I knew would not dance but would enjoy me saying hi to her. I walked next to the child who had been declared mute, although I was convinced he was not. This lasted no more than three minutes, and I instructed them to take their seats. I connected and reset the energy of the room. My observer had looked pleasantly surprised upon entering and observed the rest of my lesson. During the follow-up coaching conversation, she said *"You are a Natural Born Teacher"*. Tears welled in my eyes. This was my second observation. And if a veteran educator was saying this to me, I had to pay attention. The year 2020 has not changed the power of music. One of the easiest things in the world to do is to ask kids what songs they like and play them. Period.

I have been doing this since day one and it works. Not all the kids will respond to the same music! Fantastic! Do you know how much music there is in the world? You absolutely have to set some limits to your selection. But this is a no-brainer. My Daily Gemstone Meditation videos feature student requests. To not take away class time, no more than two minutes of the song is played. If you are in person, why not play music as you set up for the next class and kids transition? Kids can have days of the week where their song is played. I have cajoled students into coming to class with, *"Your song is being played today!"* And mind you, I hated that song! But it was school-appropriate and my kids liked it. It is about them, not me.

Note, I will never play music that is offensive or demonic. If it is in another language I do research. If I had to do too much research, it gets skipped! As a trained singer I also take time to sing to my students. I have peers who are musicians and they play or show videos of their work. If you are an artist, show your latest piece and explain what inspired your creation! Did you cook something amazing or build a chair? Share! Creation is Inspiring.

## Motivational Videos

I am a visual learner. Lights, camera, and action stimulate me, as well as engaging vocal performances. Put those two together and you have a dope motivational video!

Bishop Alexis A. Thomas is my Bishop and Spiritual Father. He was the pastor of Pilgrim Rest Baptist Church in Phoenix, Arizona from the age of 16 to his homegoing at age 50 in 2018. His influence on my life is unquantifiable. Videos of his preaching sustained me. But I could not play Baptist sermons in my public school class! But I did not give up! I found the Hip Hop Preacher Dr. Eric Thomas!

*"Waddup Waddup Waddup! It's ya boy ET and it's time for another - bring it from the bottom - Thank God It's Monday!"*

I have been hooked, locked, loaded, and a part of the tribe ever since. I used ET's TGIM (Thank God It's Monday) series to help inspire my kids. At first, it was just the video - then I incorporated the body. Everyone had to stand up and stretch and say it. To differentiate, they can say *"Thank Goodness it's Monday"* or *"Thank ___ it's Monday!"* I know my audience so I adjust accordingly. ET's energy is electrifying. And I may not have it in me every morning. But I can always push play! The titles of ET's videos can help you curate the experience you need for the day. If your kids are doing well, don't play the TGIM *Take me to your Bedroom* as ET admonishes people for being fake. Play the TGIM *You Are Amazing* since that is uplifting and gets kids on board. You need to connect before you correct.

Furthermore, there is a litany of other calm or hype videos you can play excerpts of to support your students. Instrumental videos of smooth jazz were effective during independent work time with my co-teacher. The instrumental of Hamilton's *"My Shot"* was played when students were doing group work for their own rap battle presentation. Different times can call for different kinds of inspirational music and videos. Before the lesson about election day, play the country song *"Undivided"* by Tim McGraw, it is so dope!

## Quote Cards

A quote that puts things in perspective can also give students of different behavior styles what they need to be inspired. Perhaps instead of the video mediation, it is a mantra meditation for a silent two minutes. During one rendition of my meditation time, I wrote a word or mantra on a notecard and gave one to each child. A few examples are below.

*"You are a King", "You are Kind", "You are Love", "Believe in Yourself, Skinner thinks you're Amazing", "You have no Clue how awesome you are", "I see how hard you work. It's going to pay off."*

I had 27 students in that class and I did not repeat a phrase. Students take out those cards and read/meditate on those words. Virtually, I have directly messaged students their vision or focus words. In my small class as a part of the entry routine, students write their Super Power word in the chat. Words are powerful. And our students need time to meditate on words. Positive self-talk needs to be taught. New virtual learning mantras are needed for students and teachers. These are some I've meditated on:

"You don't have to be great to get started, but you have to get started to be great." - *Les Brown*

"Everything is fine." - *Naomi Skinner (aka Mommy)*

"All is Well." - *Bishop Alexis Thomas, Sermon on the Shulammite Woman*

"You are logged in, everything is ok."

"My teachers are here for me."

"My students are here for me."

"My admin have my back."

"Wifi issues are not my fault."

"They will see that I am trying."

"I cannot be blamed for things out of my control."

"I will not focus on things out of my control."

"I can do this!"

"Let's go Diamond!" - *Martinez J. Skinner (aka Dad)*

"I can, I will, I must!" - *Dr. Eric Thomas*

"Go Be Amazing on Purpose!" - *Extreme Teachers' Director VaLarie Humphrey*

## _Do Life_ With Them

The most inspiring thing about life is living it. Show your students glimpses of how you are living this life and making it through. It does not help them if they think we are perfect. Modeling life in front of our students is the most culturally relevant, responsive, and sustaining thing we can do.

I do NOT mean telling them all of your dating business or hygiene routine, that is inappropriate and tacky. But if your alarm did not go off, tell them. If you are struggling with death in your family, tell them. If you get cranky without breakfast, tell them! If your Wi-Fi is sketchy and you understand what they are dealing with, tell them! If you are cold in this frozen building too, tell them! It will bring you and your students closer through the shared experience. You have to form relationships to know what to say and not say. But there is always a minimal way to show them that you are living this life along with them, and if you can do it, they can too!

Take notes on how students engage in your classroom. At the start of every year, I survey the students. I ask them what kind of media they partake in. I also give options for those who will say _"nothing"_. I can gauge who is ready to engage and who is more reluctant. A child may not say their music preference but you can ask them what social media platforms they are enchanted with. You should notice which kids answer which questions on the form. If you ask questions that include things like "Who are your favorite celebrities?" or "What motivates you?" or "Who are your favorite authors or athletes?" you can curate your Socioemotional Learning (SEL) techniques to fit their needs. Diversity is crucial in many formats. So you should plan ways to diversify your techniques in general.

As a Certified Extreme Teacher with Eric Thomas's organization and under the leadership of VaLarie Humphrey, I use the DISC personality assessment to help me govern my behavioral style and identify the behavior styles of students. Even without the kids taking the personality assessment for themselves, the training I receive allows me to teach and reach all students. This is the most effective way I have learned how to communicate and connect with my students and colleagues.

**GEMs**

❖ Inspiration means: the child wants to learn because you made them feel good.

❖ Use Music, Videos, Quotes, and any combination of the three.

❖ Model Life Moves, it is a part of culturally relevant pedagogy.

❖ Don't create content, repurpose content. Use what they give you and what has worked for you.

❖ Use Diamond Emerald's "Gemstones: Meditation and Motivation" Playlist free on Youtube.

❖ Become a Certified Extreme Teacher and add the DISC assessment to your teacher toolkit.

# CHAPTER 4

# N - Never Give Up

*Weebles Wobble but they don't fall down!* This was the slogan for a toy from the 1970s when my elder brother was growing up. My mother often used this slogan as a mantra when I got down on myself and felt like giving up. You do not need to search long to find people who have absconded from the education field and will encourage you to do the same. They will tell you to give up on this profession. You will not find that here.

**The "N" in "Shine Brite" stands for "Never Give Up".**

Chapter 2 established that we are all New Teachers. The only way to no longer be a New Teacher, is to keep teaching! So Never Give Up, and create systems that support you. There is supreme power in a good system. You had systems before the pandemic! You had systems before you became a teacher! Tap into them. Rate their effectiveness and reliability in different spaces. The technique "Threshold" is a <u>Teach Like a Champion</u> (TLAC) technique that teachers have been using for centuries. It involves greeting the students at the door and giving instructions for the starting activity. Virtually, this looks like me greeting each student by name and asking them to tell me how they are doing by writing a number between 1 (not great) and 5 (wonderful) in the chat. This also involves some private messaging, whereas in person I would speak to them outside of the classroom and ask them to show me the number on their hands. This could even call for a breakout room session. Just because I can no longer conduct a routine in the same way, does not mean I give up on the routine. We Never Give Up. The "Threshold' technique is about connection, which is essential especially at the start of the class. But there are many systems that teachers can rely on and/or may need to create in light of teaching in today's world.

In college at Washington University in St. Louis, I took a night class taught by Reverend Dr. Harvey Fields. He was like our own personal MLK. The class was called the *College Success Seminar*. It felt like a trick! *Wait - they're just going to tell me how to win at this private university? No way!* I could not understand how the class was open to the public and still had seats left. I and a group of friends colluded and reserved our seats! It was one of the best experiences of my undergraduate life. It did not hurt that the instructor and most of my classmates looked like me. Reverend Professor Fields taught us how to do life. I am forever grateful. A Time Management Template is one concrete system I took from his course that has served me as a teacher. It is simply a spreadsheet that forces/allows you to see how your time is allotted. We calculated the number of hours we spent in classes, sleeping, working, and eating. Then we identified how many hours of studying, reading, writing, or rehearsing (I double majored in African & African American Studies & Theatre Arts) was needed for each course. We were able to see how many extra hours in the day we *really* had, then we could hold ourselves accountable. It was no accident I graduated with Latin Honors (Magna Cum Laude) from the #12th school in the USA. I took the course, aced the course, and followed the system in real life. So why would I not bring that system into my teaching career? Now, I know leisure time was on the Time Management Template, but I did not devote much time in that area in college. As a teacher, I understand the need to have self-care and "turn off times" scheduled into your life. Especially as a New Teacher, the profession will take everything it can from you. It will suck the life out of you, and just hire someone else when you die. That teacher turnaround hurts kids. It hurts our education system. It hurts our country. It hurts our world. We need resilient, dynamic educators who have systems in place and who maintain their systems.

**<u>Thou must check thyself before thy wreck thyself.</u>**

Another system that I use is an electronic Dashboard. Guess what, it is another spreadsheet! The idea behind this Dashboard is to create tabs with different work products on them. In our case, they are different classes and each tab has an objective or class you are taking notes on. The main page is the homepage where big picture things are stored. The Dashboard is pertinent for my work as a special educator. We have too many paperwork checks and balances to cover as special education providers. Mistakes that cost schools money are dependent upon us performing the correct procedural task promptly. Your name/file number is attached to every keystroke you make. Making any mistakes can cost your school money, cost a child to not receive a service they need, and ultimately cost you your job. God forbid any Special Educator think they do not need a system! I had one, but it proved broken and needed maintenance. School closures were a great time to do maintenance work on our systems.

We have even *more* paperwork to do to accommodate for the hybrid teaching shifts. Every single child who received special education services had to have their IEP (Individualized Education Pan) paperwork updated. That work was not allocated equally amongst school staff. It was the special education providers, paraprofessionals, psychologists, counselors, IEP teachers, ESL, TESOL, OT,/PT, Speech providers (and more) who had to handle this work. So one of the ways we help each other is by sharing our systems. My fellow providers have skills and expertise I do not. One is a whiz at tracking and producing data for science. Another is great at creating the templates for emails we should send to our parents. The other is our leader and creates the calendar and color codes documents to streamline communication. One is a small group guru and always follows up with strategies that work for our 8th graders. Yet another is the math specialist and provides goals that are aligned to standards and can check our work. Because of my schedule, I tend to know and teach all of the kids who have IEPs and I serve as the social studies expert.

I personally needed to add an accountability partner along with my Dashboard since it did not suffice. Now, once I color code the spreadsheet, I also email/text/call my co- provider and friend and tell her once I have completed a task. She congratulates me and everyone wins! Her job is done since she also happens to be the IEP teacher and in charge of paperwork compliance. Better yet, we are friends and have a strong working relationship since we teach the same students and have the same struggles. Finally, we are helping the school by having more sets of eyes on this important aspect of our bureaucracy, that is connected to our state funding. And when schools are funded, kids win. That is dynamic teaching. One answer to the demands of hybrid teaching is not to abandon your systems but to rework them, use them, and maintain the systems. Creating a system that helps you stay afloat will decrease the likelihood of you giving up.

## Missing Kids

One of the more heartbreaking aspects of hybrid teaching is the loss of some of our kids. I do not mean figuratively, I mean literally. The day we went remote was the last day I communicated with some of my students. They were unable to log on. They did not show up for classes. They did not complete the work. If they turned in assignments they were blank. Some showed no signs of life at all. Some were 8th graders so I literally saw nothing past March 2020. That hurts. But we must Never Give Up on reaching out to our students that are not showing up.

Each school has an attendance procedure and protocol for how to mark students absent. To attack this problem, some teachers are in charge of reaching out directly, others have attendance teachers who are assigned this duty, and some tasks can be given to paraprofessionals or school aides. But at the end of the day, during your class period, you are responsible. That means even if your co-teacher is documenting the absence, you should be aware of it and have a system to follow up. With my co-teachers, we take turns taking attendance and following up with missing students. I am skilled at sending warm and urgent emails to get kids to class like:

*Subject: URGENT - We're Missing You!*
*Body: We have SS now! (insert link)*
*Skinner*

or

*Subject: SS NOW!*
*Body: We're working on the essay- I really want to help you*
*with this! Join now! (insert link)*
*Skinner*

The goal of the email is to invite them, to entice them to join the class. The goal is not to admonish them for being late but give them another chance to be successful. If they miss class, they get a follow-up email with the link to my office hours for the day. While it may be a bit more cumbersome to insert the link, it is increasing the likelihood of the child coming to class. And, is that not the goal? If we are really about our business, we can create the system and have the draft of the emails ready before the day starts! If you know who tends to be late, cue up the emails in advance, and let them surprise you! It feels GREAT when I am about to email a kid and they pop up in the waiting room. And once they get there, if they are a social person, I will greet them aloud or in the chat with a *"Hey Charlie glad you made it!"* But, most likely, if they are on the "late list" they will not desire that attention. I will always privately message them *"I'm so glad you made it"*. We have been doing this for a year. I have had this system for probably 8 months. Most of them do not reply to that message. But I send it anyway. Why? They could have read it. And I need them to know they are an important part of this community.

Similarly, with the assistance of other teachers and administrators, I have started a wake-up call system called "Gemstone Wake Up Calls". I get the contact information for the students I teach who are "chronically absent". In addition, as a support for the school, I have access to the list of students school-wide who are "chronically absent" or late to first period. My job was to fix that. I cannot fix something I cannot track. The data I was given allowed me to see the varying degrees of truancy. Moreover, we had other data collection points. My school does listening conferences and whatever the parent reports is made available to teachers. I was given access to the students' grade reports for that year so I could assess if they were skipping any classes, or if it was just the first period. I also have access to IEP data. The "chronically absent" list, the "students who receive services" list, the "free and reduced lunch list", and the "diversity initiative" list .... Do I have to say it? Academic comorbidity is real.

All those lists look alike. But you know what? I have been on some of those lists. And I know how to intervene in the lives of those on those lists. That is my Superpower. So I created a page on my electronic Dashboard and dedicated it to the "Gemstone Wake up Calls". I identify from the data kids I may be able to connect with. I do not choose students who I know already have someone intervening in their lives. I do not pick more kids than I feel I can handle on this type of caseload (12-15max). I do pick kids my administrators have asked about specifically and those whose data stands out to me, or the spirit of discernment calls me to.

The protocol went like this: initial emails or texts were sent to the children & parents informing them of my intervention. It was light and positive. I mentioned I was another support, that I wanted to connect with the child, and invited them to reply "Hi" to my initial email. The initial template was standard and included the "Gemstone Daily Meditation" video I had made for the day. If students were texting they also got a Bitmoji! I kept track daily to ensure I did reach out to each student I was supposed to. I tracked the method and if they replied or not. Some students provided both phone numbers and emails, I did not want to keep both forms of communication, I felt that was extra. Therefore, I have to check my systems to see which ones they responded to. One student wanted to be texted but it took him two weeks to get in the habit of keeping his phone charged. Now that we have a system I no longer email him.

The messages will start to become differentiated. After the first week parents no longer get the email (unless the admin has requested that intervention). Some students are asked to reply "Hi", some are given the next level and asked what songs they enjoy so they can be added to the "Gemstone Mediations" I create. I may ask them to respond on a scale of 1-5 about how they are feeling. If they have been missing class or not attending their speech or SETSS (special education teacher support services) sessions, I'll ask them to attend my office hours (the parents are added on these emails) and the link is provided. I always ask for some type of confirmation and I make it clear. *"Reply Yes or No if you will be at office hours"* or *"Reply "Hi" and let me know you are awake and ready for the first period."*

The most successful interventions involve parent meetings. We reset expectations and focus on communication and showing up. I have seen "chronically absent" students show up on time for class 5 days in a row! Not all kids need or can have that family meeting. I have still seen that for some students the morning check-ins are enough to correlate to increased attendance.

The "N" stands for "Never Give Up" because some of these kids straight ghosted me! But I do not care! I have a job to do and lives to save! Ten years from now, they will not be able to say that Skinner gave up on them. They will not be able to say their middle school did not reach out to them. I know them ignoring me is not personal. Some of these students I am reaching out to have never seen me. Some of these students are caring for alcoholic parents and couldn't care less about my Bitmojis. But when someone checks my records, they will see that that student was invited to office hours and alternative class times consistently. I have receipts. I take pride in loving hard. And, when that kid finally reads my email or hears my voice message, or watches that video, they will not hear condemnation. The reason I care about the missing assignments is that it indicates my student is missing out on life. Maybe they are missing assignments because they do not understand Google Classroom. Or, maybe they do not understand how to write complete sentences. Regardless, I will not find out if I am harping on about the missing assignments in my communications. When a student ignores me or logs off a Zoom call in the middle of our conversation, my first words in the email are *"are you ok"*? I assume the best because things could be the worst. I Never Give Up, because that may be what they are used to. With all the changes that are taking place, we have to model what it looks like to Never Give Up.

## Track Academic Growth or Academic Death

*"Kids can't learn due to COVID.19",* said the weak teacher. Mindset shift alert! The news is saying one thing, the Teacher's Union is saying another, the parents are saying a third. But whose report will you believe? What decisions will you make about your belief system? If we acquiesce and accept this notion, we have lost already. I have come to the true realization that at the end of the day all that matters is what happens in the locus of my classroom. The state may want me to do a twenty-minute segment of single-digit multiplication review. How I structure those twenty minutes is up to me. It does not need to be consecutive, it could be four five-minute activities within the lesson. It could include Socratic questioning and error analysis. It could include team activities and competition. Virtual or in person.

Before hybrid teaching began we blamed the 45th President and racism for stunting the growth of our students. We called it the Opportunity Gap. The true gaps that need to be closed are the ones amongst teachers, students, and parents. The 45th President was never in your classroom running anything! What a Blessing! The growth and lack thereof of your students was in your hands. Guess what, it still is! You are still the Boss Teacher! The virus has not stopped you! We cannot give in to the mindset of defeat and surrender. It is heartbreaking and it is unacceptable that we have lost contact with some of our students. We acknowledge the hurt, then we act to address it.

Some of my students are significantly behind. Teachers that "Shine Brite" do not panic, we pivot. How did we work with struggling students before? Strategic intervention with Specially Designed Instruction. SDI is the delivery method of special education services. What I teach at the university level is how to track and sustain academic growth in students in a 1:1 tutoring setting. I now conduct PDs at schools and support teachers in doing the same thing through a pandemic and out of a pandemic.

## GEMs

- ❖ Never Give Up: Means that we lean on our systems and create new systems to sustain us.

- ❖ Lean back on paper systems and/or systems that have supported you in the past (hint - you graduated college!)

- ❖ Thou must check thyself before thy wreck thyself.

- ❖ Use systems to track and locate missing students.

- ❖ Track Academic Growth or Academic Death

# CHAPTER 5

# E · Energy

Light has energy. Different types of light carry different types of energy and power. Yet, they both shine. The light of a book lamp will suffice for finishing that assignment. But a targeted laser light can eliminate cancer cells. Dynamic teachers need to use their laser focused energy to eliminate the cancer of apathy in education. Energy is one of the most important resources we have as teachers, it is free, but it must be wielded and protected. It must be used in a way that is positive and powerful.

## The "E" in "Shine Brite" stands for Energy!

Teachers compete against the latest technology and the latest trends in social media, the virtual world, and the physical world! Good teaching always includes engaging students and capturing their attention. We as human beings have energy that we need to skillfully distribute throughout the day. Dynamic teaching involves restructuring your energy in person and virtually.

Creating positive energy in your lessons is a crucial component. This will support students and support your emotional and physical health. It is our job to create positive energy in our classroom especially when the world has devolved into negativity. What follows are the techniques myself and other dynamic, diamond teachers employ to hone and focus our energy.

## Quick is Queen

Changing the pace of your lessons is the most straightforward way to vary the energy flow of your class. A slow pace does not always indicate a lack of energy. On the contrary, high-energy moments can take place during slow-paced activities. In addition, going from a slow pace to an energetic activity is a wonderful way to add excitement to your lessons. Thoughtful planning is key. The idea behind the Quick is Queen technique is to implement short bursts of engagement that check for understanding and add energy to the class.

I start my class with a "Gemstone Meditation" video which could be described as a slower-paced or calming activity. While the meditation is individual, immediately after the video I ask kids to do something quickly that brings them back into the group. If the featured song in the Gemstone was *"What a Wonderful World"* by Louis Armstrong, I might say *"Put a W in the chat if you want to feel Wonderful."* Or *"drop a 3 in the chat if you're ready to move on!"* That allows engagement even if the kid did not like the song! This technique works because it gives students something concrete to do. It allows all levels of students to engage in the task. It is time-bound and does not take away from the lesson. It re-engages the student who may not have been at the computer or attentive at the time. This can also be done in person. In-person I would lean on verbal engagement and physical demonstrations.

## Call and Response

This technique is one of my cultural strengths and as such makes me very comfortable. The idea behind call and response is the same virtually or in person. Have students engage by repeating a phrase, posing a hypothetical question to a peer, or doing anything else to demonstrate an *"Amen"!*

For instance, *"Repeat after me 'I love my life'"* after the song, "I love my Life" by Demarco plays. Or *"If you're ready say 'ready!'"*. However, to manage my energy and to serve all students I can always give options for non-verbal engagement. It is not a good use of energy, nor is it positive, to wait for all students to respond verbally. There is a multitude of reasons they may not respond (refer back to "The Camera Issue" and think of this as "The Mic Issue").

And as a way of life, I need to be open to failure. There are definitely times when I ask, and students refuse to repeat, I note it and move on. I have to know my audience. Despite the relationship we have developed, I have students who would not "repeat after me" if their life depended on it! Not out of disrespect, but for a litany of other reasons that range from cultural differences to disability manifestations. Still, Call and Response is a method of formative assessment that can even be tracked on the Dashboard you have created.

I would then try nonverbal measures: *"Write a 'W' in the upper left corner of your paper"* or *"Show me the sign we use to represent social aspects of culture"*. Then I would await the physical gesture (which is to hug oneself), then model the gesture, then move on. Using Call and Response is a time-tested teacher technique. Figure out how to adapt it for online learning. I have had kids review vocabulary words online by performing this technique. *"Unmute and say "Militarism"*. My co-teacher has even added to this and says *"We see 22 students on this call so we should see 22 mics unmute and hear 22 voices."* Similarly, if I am requesting engagement in the chat I might say *"I'm looking for your vote yes or no. I'm still looking for 17 responses since there are 18 people on this call besides myself."* Then, affirm and thank students for their work.

Shout out students who are doing the heavy lifting. This also can change the energy flow of your classroom and encourage those who have checked out, to get some praise from us and their peers.

**<u>Change who wins by changing the pace!</u>**

We all have students who would be considered eager beavers, and will answer first in the chat or verbally or both! It is our job as educators to keep that child intellectually engaged, while also ensuring they do not sacrifice the experience of others. We already know how to engage those students right? The scholar and educator Christopher Emdin mentioned how we need to create a Jeopardy-like experience in our classes. When a Jeopardy (or Kahoot) game is being played in class, students are all the way live and the pace is quick and electrifying! School now becomes exciting since they can actually accrue points in a live way. The amount of excitement and engagement students get out of working in teams and getting content questions correct can cause students to erupt with the chorus of joyous wins and devastating losses!

When middle schools in New York City closed at the end of a workday on Wednesday all teachers had to pivot! The random closing and opening of schools in a pandemic creates chaotic energy. It is hard to regulate one's energy when you are unsure of when and how to properly apply it since conditions are in constant flux. In my social studies class, that week we engaged in a Jeopardy game that reviewed content for the upcoming assessment. The categories we covered in the Native New York unit were displayed at the top: *Indigenous People, Geography, Enslavement, Colonization, & Sourcing.* Students then select their category and point level of the question. This is a multi-faceted assessment!

Since the students choose their category, I get to see what parts of the unit they feel successful in and where they see limitations. This is also an assessment of my teaching. I can see what targets I successfully addressed and which ones I missed. I can now align my future energy to addressing their gaps in the unit. Furthermore, although schools closed, my team was ready to perform Jeopardy during our Zoom class without skipping a beat. One of my coworkers has been using Kahoot for years. So it was natural for him to translate this quiz game to online platforms. We used our energy planning lessons/techniques that would be feasible in person and or for an online transition.

During this new phase of education, we must regulate our energy as we could be transferred to any setting at any time. We need to take advantage of the online tools, while also being ready to give them up at a moment's notice! Use PD or preps to research and try out your preferred (or mandated) online platforms. Pick your backup go-to system. Online educational gaming platforms should be used by every teacher. It should be a crucial part of your Teacher Toolkit. At the point of writing, Flocabulary is my go-to resource which also has assessments built-in. These change extremely quickly but as of now, teachers have used Nearpod, Peardeck, Bitmoji Classrooms, Edgenuity, Desmos, and other online platforms with a curriculum built-in. Even if you do not love them and they are not differentiated enough for your students, you must have one on your side! Even if all these platforms go out of business or raise their prices out of our limits, we can still email our students! These are prime opportunities to teach real-life skills of online communication with students in new ways.

## Design Class Activities with Energy in Mind

Changing the pace of your class can help students who rarely win, win in your classroom. Quick short responses are great for some students. Taking time and pouring out their knowledge at the end of a lesson is great for other students. From my hundreds of conversations with students, they have given me insight into their experiences with remote learning. Students report that having to perform multiple times in a period can be exhausting and overwhelming. Can we not relate? Be mindful of what you are asking of students and what is *most* important. I stated previously that I start by asking students to respond to the "Gemstone Meditation". While this is data for me, this is not a measure of if they have conquered the standards for the lesson. If a child *only* participates in the Exit Ticket, that is still a success. I must be mindful that I teach a variety of little human beings. So, the Exit Ticket I design must be standards-aligned. Furthermore, I have had students who can and willingly participate in the live lesson, but bail on the Exit Ticket. So the lesson activities I design must *also* be standards-aligned!

Call out students for how they engage and praise those who are motivated by this. Recently a student wrote in the chat that they were not sure how to answer the question. I was very very excited to see this! This is a student who never turns their camera on and rarely participates overall. I immediately praised him publicly for participating! I said *"Timmy is already winning today! I know he is having trouble with the question, but I know he is here! Keep listening and see what people write in the chat. Thanks for getting us started!"* When I said aloud that this child was winning he wrote in the chat *"I am? Yes!"* Furthermore, after going through the answers of his peers, he added a correct answer to the chat. Fully bridging that circle of assessment, positive affirmations, and academic growth. I asked a question he could not answer, I praised his participation then gave him skills to be successful (listen/read and adjust your answer), waited for the revision, and praised the end result.

This class activity (question and answer session) was designed with medium to high energy in mind. Students had to write sentences in the chat to convey their answers. Waiting for the answer formation slows down the pace of the class. Asking students to revise their answers slows the pace of the class, but also gives those who need more time to craft better answers after seeing/hearing the eager beavers take a whack at it!

## Project Based Learning

Project Based Learning is a wonderful way for students to demonstrate their skills and abilities in a synthesized way. Rather than addressing one question or skill, projects allow students to habit stack and show connections between ideas. Yet, this requires a child/person to sustain their energy over long periods of time. They must come back to a problem/task over multiple days. This requires lessons that have some type of daily accountability. For instance, I design the Black History Month projects for my department each year. We meet and we discuss our goals and concerns. I then assess the world and help identify what could/should be addressed. Then I align the work to the standards. Students work in groups for a little over a week to collectively assemble a creative and informative presentation. In order to support the energy output, there are daily forms students complete to assess their work output for the day. At the culmination of the project students present and write a reflection that overviews the work. Some students had trouble producing energy at the end of each lesson and did not complete the forms. I worked to pop into breakout groups and write privately to students to get them credit for the work they did. Some students were able to fill out the daily forms and it supported their cohesive submission of the project. After the live presentation of the project, students had a final opportunity to demonstrate their knowledge by writing a paragraph to summarize their learning. This could have also been done verbally for those students with writing limitations. Choice Boards & Tic Tac Toe game boards are also ways to allow students to regulate their own energy over multiple days (independently or in a group) resulting in a final project.

## Manage your Own Energy!

There is a litany of things that we cannot control as teachers. We do not control what time school starts and ends, if kids have their cameras on or off, or if vaccines are required. We cannot control what classes we teach in, whom we teach with, what students we serve, or when our lunch is. We cannot control the number of students allowed in a room for social distancing. We cannot control if the virtual platforms work that day or not. We cannot control if students show up or not. I refuse to even continue this list because it is taking Energy! **Don't spend Energy on things you cannot control.** We expend different Energy at the start of the school year than before the winter break. We extend different Energies during the end of the marking period or during field trips. There are seasons to teaching. The pandemic has revealed different seasons like Zoom/Google Meets fatigue. It has brought the season of re-entries and closures. It has brought the season of mourning and celebration. Spot the season as soon as you can - and adjust accordingly. This means fighting only the battles you can win. And when you fail, take a minute to get rejuvenated and Bounce Back (more on this in Chapter 6)!

## Breathe

Changing the pace of your class can support Socioemotional Learning and combat the trauma students have been facing. As a social studies teacher, I have the privilege of discussing difficult topics with children. As a teacher, we all have the responsibility to be responsive to our students and the world around us. No teacher has the right to "just teach their content" and ignore everything else. Current events affect our students, and caring for students is our job. This does not mean your AP Calc course is now a current events course. But if nothing else, state the issue (or let a student) and take a moment to breathe. As I lead students in my Gemstone meditation-videos *"take a deep breath in and let it out"*. You can also allow them to do this without you. *"Take a private 60 seconds to breathe through your emotions and thoughts. Afterwards, we will return to our lesson."* It also helps remind students that we are human and we too are affected. This is not forcing anyone to engage who is not ready, but it also allows the child who is feeling vulnerable to take a beat - before moving on.

Because - we will move on - that is our job.

The paradox of schools is that we must be a safe haven from the world, and the means by which students process the world. We have to simultaneously be available for conversation, while also allowing students to forget the evils that exist in their homes or communities. Taking time to breathe helps us balance this space. If a student is not ready to move on, or having an emotional moment or breakdown, that is where we tag in our guidance counselors. But before you ignore current events, before you assume that a child has not experienced as much trauma as another, breathe. Then be brave enough to shift your energy.

**GEMs**

* ❖ Energy does not just mean being "excited" but injecting different energy flows into your lessons to support different student needs.

* ❖ Energy does not mean exerting all your strength at all times, it means managing your energy for different seasons of teaching to avoid teacher burnout!

* ❖ Lean on Techniques you have used before and adapt them for your current students and setting.

* ❖ Lastly, Breathe.

# CHAPTER 6

# B - Bounce Back & Fail Forward

Teaching is the business of failure. Failure is a necessary component of success. Failure solidifies and reinforces learning. To fear failure is to fear growth. To fear failure is to fear success. To Fear failure is to fear teaching. Every day, whether we know it or not, we are engaged in a struggle between failure and success. I am one of the best teachers on the planet, because of all my failures. We have to be willing to fail in order to win. Facets are cuts that make Diamonds. Each facet, each cut, must be implemented in exact ways to reveal each diamond's fire and brilliance! Each facet, in each failure, we must Bounce Back & Fail Forward to reveal each dynamic diamond teacher's fire and brilliance!

**The "B" in "Shine Brite" stands for "Bounce Back & Fail Forward".**

Hybrid teaching invariably created new ways for us to fail! How annoying is that? No - how exciting is that?! If I know the ways to fail, I can also know the ways to win! This hybrid teaching world came with a litany of unknowns. We are still living in the litany of unknowns. Allow me to spend some time here to reveal some failures we know about, and how to Bounce Back from them.

## Zoom Bombing

Definition: An assailant gains entry into your virtual classroom and interrupts in some way. This can be as minimal as silently entering under a student's name and recording the session for future negative use. This can be as invasive as taking control of the class and broadcasting pornography on the screen. The gap in between these realities includes annotating on the screen offensive messages or drawings, or unmuting and yelling offensive attacks, or doing so in the chat.

Fail Forward: This is one of the most hurtful attacks on a teacher and their learning environment. We have protocols in the school building prohibiting strangers from entering the building, let alone invading our classroom. Now - every Tom, Dick, and Harry can potentially pull up in the room causing serious trauma for all involved. To Fail Forward (to react in the moment) I lean on the advice given to me by my peers and my own experience. You are the master of that ship and the captain of that classroom at all times. *Do not forget it.* You must stay steady at the helm. Depending on the interruption, always start by addressing it sternly and making your standards clear. This starts with taking attendance and admitting people into the space. Do you have the "waiting room" feature setup? You must! Once this is done, does your school have a domain name unique to your students? If so, change the Zoom settings so only those authorized email addresses are admitted to your room. The person must log in to that email account to gain access. When you admit students ensure they have their names spelled correctly. Any misspellings could indicate a poser trying to get in your room. Participants should not be allowed to change their names. This ensures the email address and the people are one and the same. You can admit students into the room one at a time. Then you can verify their identity by having them speak or turn on their camera.

This takes an exorbitant amount of time. So this should only be done in the first or second class to establish protocols. Another tip is to admit them all at once and require cameras on and/or a verbal attendance check. The chat alone is *not* sufficient to verify the identity of a student when you are dealing with Zoom bombing. I suggest admitting them all at once and spending the Do Now/Meditation time to verify attendance and identity. If there is someone not responding, I will announce their name up to three times before removing them from the room. Check your Zoom features. You can either decide that when you remove a child, they cannot return, or set it up so they can. Check with your admin or tech team to decide what is best for your school. Your school should have systems and protocols that govern these interactions. Yet, every teacher needs to cover their own business. When Zoom bombing happens, it is YOUR JOB to Fail Forward. End the call. Start a new Zoom/Meets session with a new Zoom link if there is more than 20min left of class.

Bounce Back:

It happened - now what? Apologize to your students. If you are able to, get onto another Zoom call directly after the incident. Apologize quickly, establish your dominance, and keep it moving. Do not give the incident more power than it has already taken from your class. Ignorance and bad things happen in the world. That does not change what work needs to be done. Model resilience! This will be more of a lesson to them than whatever you were teaching. Be clear that what happened was not ok and explain why. Set a moral precedent. And if it was someone in the community, something as simple as *"Consequences will be given to people who do not respect themselves or our community. No one has the right to do what just took place in our space"*.

The administration should be informed immediately so they can begin to take the actions needed to address the parents/and or school community at large. Never send a disciplinary type of email without consulting with the admin. The next virtual class should feel a bit different. Perhaps you go back to admitting kids one by one into the meetings until you feel safe again. Perhaps you ask an admin or co-teacher to join to keep things safe. But what you cannot do, is no longer show up for your kids and teach in the way you did before. Maybe now you go harder and are more strategic since you know how precious that time and space are! Maybe the fear of Zoom Bombing will make you make better use of the virtual time you have since it could be stolen away. They can try to bomb if they want to, bomb back by ensuring your class can recover from a virtual invasion!

## Teaching Fails

Definition: Trying to teach a lesson that worked in person, but it does not work online or vice versa. Any planned move that does not go as planned.

Fail Forward: This is a super broad category but the overall response is the same. The idea behind Failing Forward is planning ahead knowing failure is coming. It is naive to believe that the same implementation of a lesson exists in-person, or hybrid, or with masks. The same content can be taught, but you must plan for things we cannot plan for. For instance, my social studies department must deliver the same lesson to all students both in person, and remote, delivered by three instructors. One teacher is all remote, one teacher is all in person, and one teacher is hybrid (me). It would have been naive for the department head to believe that no modifications needed to be made, so he always made time for that planning during meetings. Something we could not plan for was how exactly attendance would be taken and how long it would take. In-person teachers must retrieve students in one location and escort them in socially distanced lines to another location. Spaces and hands need to be sanitized in advance, during and after every act. If a student is late this throws off all the safety procedures and your attendance protocol. I stopped in my tracks the first time a student came late to my in-person post-pandemic classroom. My mind began to race.

*Did they use the right doors? Did they touch anything? Is that an approved mask? Did they sign the waiver? I cannot see their face - Who IS THAT CHILD? What desk are they going to? Did they walk the approved pathway? Are they keeping their distance? Are they going to hand me something? I don't want to touch it! Are they going to the right desk? Did I clean that desk? Did the custodians use their cleaning spray? How much should the window be open? Can this late kid sit near the window? Why are they late? Wait - what am I teaching?*

By the time all these questions passed through my head the child was sitting at a desk ready for me to get going! Idle time is a teaching fail. Not knowing the social distancing protocols, is a teaching fail. The first time in a social distance setting when a student asked me to go to the bathroom my response was "I ... don't ... know". And we looked at each other confused. Teaching fail.

Teaching for an extended period of time with either your camera or mic off, is a teaching fail. Trying to play a video that will not work is a teaching fail. Slideshows or activities not working in the moment is a teaching fail. The failures become more monumental when they involve children not learning. These are not the big fails that cost your license or dignity. These are the daily glitches that come with teaching. The projector bulb breaks, the copier stops working, you do not have enough markers because Mike sneezed on one last period and you let him keep it, etc.

So nothing has really changed about that. Good News! This should also help you keep calm, bulbs been breaking before hybrid teaching! A blank screen share or no audio on a video is nothing new. You will still be an amazing teacher.

Bounce Back:

It happened - now what? When that poor child wanted to go to the bathroom, this was nowhere in my lesson plan. My brain began to scroll through all the recent emails, but this was taking too long! So I stopped my thoughts and started my feet. I put one foot into the hallway (and one in my class per protocol) and sought help! The guidance counselor came to my rescue! Very appropriate if I might add! She escorted my student to the bathroom where she waited in line for single entry usage. Pre-covid there were no escorts, pre-covid there were no lines in the halls. I had to ask for help. Instead of trying to rationalize anything like I did the first time, I stopped my head and moved my feet. This could also translate to stopping my head and moving my hands to find the email with the bathroom protocols. This could also translate to stopping my head and moving my mouth to direct a student to *"Stop! You must keep your distance even in the classroom. Please do not walk back and forth to the trash can"*. It was disheartening to say the last statement. But I could not risk the child breaking a rule that would get him removed from the in-person learning experience. To Bounce Back from many teaching fails, just ask for help from other teachers!

For activity teaching fails, your lesson should be planned with multiple activities and access points. So if task one isn't working just move on with the lesson. You can also vary the length of time you would have spent on an activity.

If the Nearpod task is not working, abort it and spend more time in breakout rooms. If the breakout room feature is not working how you want it, pivot and perform the task whole-group or allow students to write in the chat. Be creative and assign kids to work alone then join you for a whole group discussion or 1:1. Ask them! Students are very creative and resilient. You need to find at least one kid in every class that is on your team. If you can get engagement from one, leverage it and honor it. They are the ones to ask *"Hey Shayna! Give me a thumbs up if you can see and hear the video."* You avoid failing again by checking in with students often. You check explicitly about what you need and how you want them to engage. It would be a fail to ask students to raise their Zoom hands when they are unaware of how, or why they are doing so. I make sure I do not fail by asking everyone to raise their Zoom hand at the start of class. Before asking students to annotate or fill out a form as a task, I ensure they know how to annotate and/or complete the task. Students will tell you what is working and what is not. Are you listening?

To Bounce Back from many other teaching fails, just ask for help from your students!

## **Parent Fails**

Definition: Any breakdown of communication between the teacher and parent/guardian.

Fail Forward: This is another broad category but the heart of the matter is the same. We teach Other People's Children as Lisa Delpit so aptly put it. That title alone shook me and should shake you back from any negative feelings you have about children. The pandemic has exacerbated feelings of isolation and also feelings of loyalty. It has torn families apart and brought families together. Hybrid learning has increased the likelihood that we have not made visual contact with families. This makes the chance for miscommunication even greater! My voice pierces the soul, my smile is disarming and sincere and my aurora and body language is inviting. I am magnanimous in my approach and that needs to be conveyed in some way. However, virtually I have little control over how families engage with my content. I can send a video along with the email, but it is their choice to watch it or not. I can write clear and welcoming messages in English, but it may not translate completely in other languages. The way parents choose to engage with us is out of our control.

Parents listen in on our lessons and critique our teaching style or language choice. They observe the worksheets/websites and how we stumble. They see the missing/late assignments and how each teacher has their own system and they want us to fix it all. Some feel they are only reached out to when a problem arises, and that you, teacher, do not have their back. Teachers have been called out for down-talking kids, teaching virtual classes in various environments, not teaching correctly, and have even been Zoom bombed by parents! How difficult is it to teach while also fielding dissatisfaction emails/calls from parents? This breakdown could have been a discipline issue, attendance, or a missing assignment. The breakdown happened and negative feelings have been expressed from the parent to you.

Bounce Back:

It happened - now what? Apologize & Forgive. I will say that again. Apologize & Forgive. Now to whom, is up to you, but I promise it is paramount for this process. One of the failures that hurt me the most involved a parent critiquing how I spoke to their child. The attendance issue does not hurt me, nor do missing/late assignments, and even critiques of the content I take in good stride. But when the parents of one of my favorite students felt I embarrassed their child, I was mortified. To be honest I was pissed. My first response was *"is this the first time you've heard me?"*. Which was NOT the correct one. I was able, however, to formulate the correct response. The only correct one was *"I'm so sorry you and the child experienced that. It was not my intention. Please forgive me."* Mind you, I spent much more time explaining how *"this was a misunderstanding and we need to be on the same team".* I followed up with context for the moment in full and even sent a screenshot of a positive interaction we had during the same class. Now that was extra. But I was extra hurt. Furthermore, as the case manager for this student's IEP (Individualized Education Program), it was even more imperative that I mend this relationship. The parent responded generously, accepting my apology even saying *"it's all water under the bridge".* I followed up with the student by privately messaging them during the next Zoom call and ensuring they forgave me too. Between the initial email and their response, I had to spend time in meditation and prayer forgiving myself. I hate making mistakes. And this one hurt a child's feelings, so much so that mom got involved. That hurts. In the same week, another mom was texting me thanking me for intervening with her daughter. A child who was on the "chronically absent" list started showing up because of me! This teaching life is a rollercoaster. I have to forgive myself and even apologize to myself for getting depressed about my failure. The same day you fail with one, you can win with a ton.

I have been in situations where the parents are just completely wrong. I did not owe them an apology for me, but I did apologize for whatever and whoever mistreated them in the past to cause them to mistreat me. Other times when the parents cut me deep, I had to look in the mirror and apologize to and for myself.

*"I'm sorry they did that to you Diamond. You did not deserve that. And I know they should apologize but they won't or can't. But you are still a*

*good teacher. You are still a good person. And I forgive you for crying like a baby. We needed that. It's a part of the Bounce Back".*

The Bounce Back is like a trampoline, you cannot reach your full potential height without being willing to fall a little deeper than where you started.

**GEMs**

- ❖ Failure is a part of Teaching.

- ❖ Fail Forward means creating systems that prevent known failures.

- ❖ Bounce Back means to address the issue with Love, and tighten the systems.

- ❖ Asking for help, apologies, and forgiveness is paramount for this process.

# CHAPTER 7

# R - Real Recognize Real

Some teachers think that if a topic is not related to their certification field they should not talk about it. Absolutely not! It is our job to be interdisciplinary and current. *"Students don't care about what you know until they know how much you care."* This teacher adage still rings true in and out of pandemics. We cannot act like the world has not turned upside down. *"Fear has a smell,"* says Valarie Humphrey, the International Director of Extreme Teachers. Kids can smell it, and kids see through fake. Kids recognize your inner intentions and convictions. Kids can see your heart.

### The "R" in "Shine Brite" Stands for "Real Recognize Real"

We cannot ignore the summer of 2020 was a summer of sickness, and also a summer ripe with anti-blackness. On June 10th, 2020 my school community held a virtual event to address this issue. It was titled Brave Conversations 2.0. We held a similar event the year prior, and the year following. Our school district is literally in the process of desegregating. Yes, in New York City, we have some of the most segregated schools in the country. Integrated city - segregated schools. So is the city integrated? As a non-native New Yorker, I pose this question to my students. They are the experts, not me. I cannot act as if the color of their skin and mine, is not a daily part of our realities.

Being "color-blind" is inappropriate for a pedagogue. Across the country teachers, and police departments, and other government agencies have been inundated with Equity-based training. Teachers have to be taught to undo their past thinking when it comes to racial identity *and* education! The pandemic also brought to the forefront hate crimes against the Asian American and Pacific Islander communities. Ignoring these attacks and real issues only contributes to bias and hate and ignorance about the pandemic. At the start of the pandemic, an Asian identifying parent reached out to me concerned about the anti-Asian hate and gave me a resource I could share with the students. I did. That was the only correct thing to do, and I appreciated her partnership and trust in me.

## Gun Control

When the entire world is pulsing with news, we have to pay attention and be responsive to the needs and feelings of our students. This was not a new truth that started with the pandemic. School shootings prompted nationwide conversations about gun control. These conversations were polarized. The idea of arming teachers became part of daily conversations. The shooting at Marjory Stoneman Douglas High School in 2018 launched student-led protests across the country. When rumblings of our students engaging in the "March for our Lives" began to happen, the teachers had to be Real. If we ignored the issue we would have become irrelevant to our students and their lives. We spoke about the issues so our students were informed.

When they walked out of class, we did not stop them. Since the teachers belong to a Union, we could not and did not join them. However, our admin and support staff were in the streets to protect them. The students who stayed in the buildings still received intentional and standards-aligned instruction. But let's keep it real. The students who stayed in the building that day and did not join the protest happened to share something in common. They shared something in common with me. So I and my Italian co-teacher had to address what was in front of us. The brown kids, the minority, by color and by number. We had a lesson planned, but we had to be Real. Did they notice what we noticed? We asked them. And if they did not see what we saw, we said *"Why do you think the students of color are inside and the white students are outside?"* and *"Do you know what the protests were about?"* That second question was also posed to the other students the next day after the protest. Honestly, it was disheartening to hear the disparate answers to our second question from those who joined the walkout.

As a professor, I asked the teachers I taught at the University how their students and schools reacted. I had the honor of teaching a teacher who taught at the well respected, and highly supported community of Eagle Academy for Young Men. This public school consortium was created for and dedicated to educating black and brown boys in the inner city. They create a culture that is responsive to their realities, they thrive off the Real. There were no walkout protests for gun control at this teacher's Eagle Academy. In the same manner, those black and brown boys felt like their lives had been riddled with gun violence as a reality. Where was the March for *Their* Lives? So they *sat in* the class with righteous indignation. Their teachers taught with fidelity and truth. Real Recognize Real.

## Race Based Police Violence & Murders of Unarmed Black People

*"No Justice - No Peace - No Racist Police.*
*I can hear my brother saying I can't breathe*
*Again I'm in the struggle saying I can't breathe*
*We're fed up with these racist police*
*Open up your mouths and sing with me!"*

The above lines are the chorus for the song I created entitled *"Justice"* which was the featured song and music video as part of our online community intervention Brave Conversations 2.0. The event on June 10th was reminiscent of the heartbeat of our country and our community. It set the tone for what we believe in as we desegregate the school, district, city and world. Teachers must lead the way in social reform. Admin must lead the way in social reform. Children must lead the way in social reform. Parents must lead the way in social reform. All of those stakeholders were involved in our event. Equity Teams are a mandated part of every NYC public school.

Chancellor Richard Carranza led the way in Equity Training for all Department of Education public schools and was bold about *"dismantling white supremacy"*. So bold that he said these words and defended them as a Mexican American man in power. He was Real. He visited schools, and spoke to teachers with his Mariachi band alongside him! He was Real. He made mistakes in office and lost trust with teachers during the pandemic. He was Real. He was so anti-racist that white supremacist parents sued him! That was Real. He stepped down from office after losing people to the pandemic and irreconcilable differences about gifted and talented programs with the mayor. He was Real. He took a new job across the country with a private sector ed-tech company within three weeks. Is that too Real? Some people thought so. I say, talk about it with your students.

My principal is Real. He was retweeted by then Chancellor Carranza after addressing some white supremacist parents who fought (and are still fighting) against desegregating District 3 in Manhattan and District 15 in Brooklyn. My principal opened the event for us on June 10th with a speech and a picture of him at a protest proudly holding a "Black Lives Matter" sign. He is Real. There is still a litany of leaders who have yet to say this phrase. That is Real. You think kids do not notice? They do. They have told me. They have told each other. They have started their own protests. They are Real.

My principal also openly spoke to students about the pandemic from room to room before we closed on March 13th, 2020. He knew the threat was real. My Vice-Principal is an expert at people. She sees them and serves them with purpose and passion. She makes caring seem easy. She is Real. She has had numerous conversations with all the staff members collectively and individually. She has drafted over a hundred versions of the school program. That is Real. Both admin have suffered their own losses and struggles. They are Real. And they continue to lead with the best interest of their community first.

## Know thyself and deal with thyself.

The only way the above examples were able to execute their Realness is because they have a thorough understanding of themselves. What is your race? What is your racial autobiography? This is an activity I have done and taught in Professional Development sessions. You journal the story of your racial identity. Professor Henry Louis Gates (who feels like a beloved Uncle as much as I have heard, read, and seen his image) asked this question when he was in Latin America, *"When did you find out you were black"*? This question tickles me! But it is the start of your racial biography. What race are you? In the American context, you might not even know! But it is a question you must grapple with in order to uncover and face your biases.

You may not identify as Black, but your students may see you that way. That is Real. You may not identify as White, but if your students identify you that way, that is Real. This is what we mean as scholars of critical race theory when we say *"race is a social construction"*. We create it. Moreover, the students are the ones who get to decide. They decide with their language, actions, voices, and emojis! They decide with the skin tones they chose to use virtually, and the boxes they chose to check on forms. I am a Black Girl. I am a Black Girl who has been called an oreo (black on the outside and white on the inside). I am an African American who can pass as an African. That is Real. I needed to know, accept, and understand that as a person, in order to be a phenomenal teacher.

## Keep Your Promises - Good and Bad

Kids need to trust you. Dynamic diamond teachers know this and work to foster it. Students are clinging to the last touchpoint of connection they had prior to school closures. My alumni students are reaching out more than they ever have before. It is because in this virtual space they have not been able to make connections to their teachers. It is not your fault, teacher! But it is Real. Why would they trust us when their world has been turned upside down and inside out? We have to model vulnerability and tenacity (more on this later) on a regular basis. I was taught in my teacher prep program run by the NYC Teaching Fellows to always keep your promises to students. This was not in the textbook Teach Like a Champion, it was taught to me by my mother and my mentor teachers. That is why it appears in Teach like a Diamond!

Teaching, in and out of pandemics, is more than behavior management strategies and efficient routines. It involves the ebbs and flows of the science of social interaction. If you say you will call home to parents, you must. If you say you are going to give a prize for the game, you must. This is consistent. If a student is missing and you reach out to them on some consistent basis, this establishes trust. This should not be harassment! I am speaking about positive messages that allow students to reach back to a lifeline when they need it. My school's office hours are a consistent way to establish trust and be there for our students as we realize remote teaching is challenging. I had a student who was often late to school despite our school having one of the latest start times in the city. Once remote learning started it was no surprise she was consistently missing class in the mornings (or the entire day). Therefore, 1:1 social studies was administered at 4 pm for her. We did not meet for an hour, this student did not need it. She also had begun to resent the 12:1 setting she was being educated in. Yet, her chronic absenteeism prohibited her from demonstrating mastery of grade-level content. My promise was that we would meet at alternate times. I kept my promise. I was Real. She was promoted to HS. And she still checks in with me.

When you keep your promises, students have greater access to succeed.

## GEMs

- ❖ Real Recognize Real means that we respond to what happens with our authentic selves.

- ❖ Being Real means that we do not have a choice but to respond to what happens in our environment.

- ❖ It does not matter how you feel about Racial Issues, Immigration, Gun Control, LGTBQ issues, or Gifted and Talented policy changes. We are the voices of truth. Since we serve all of these communities we are responsible to them.

- ❖ Know thyself and deal with thyself! (Repeat)

- ❖ When you keep your promises, students have greater access to succeed.

# CHAPTER 8

# I - Invest in You & Them

The definition of Investing is the action or process of investing money for profit or material result. For a teacher, your financial investment should yield profit and/or academic success. In NYC, teachers are given an extra stipend in their October paycheck. This amount has ranged between $120 - $170. When I first considered going into teaching, I spoke to a current NYC Teaching Fellow in the school I was assisting in. In our first conversation, she mentioned that I would not see my friends and family during the summer of training! She then gave me a tour of her classroom, and as she pointed to various items around the room she said *"I bought that, I bought that, I bought that, I bought that,"* and she proceeded with this for about 20 different items from bulletin board borders to headphones and keyboards! At the same school, I found the IT teacher misappropriating school funds to pay for luxury items to fuel his fashion addiction and desire for designer computer bags. Regardless of these disparate extremes, teachers spend money on essential and non-essential supplies. It was part of the teaching game that I was introduced to early and often.

**The "I" in "Shine Brite" stands for "Invest in You and Them".**

I did not think twice after being accepted as an NYC Teaching Fellow when I bought an iPad to support this transition. I understood it was an investment in my craft. I still use that same iPad to this day. Despite being laughed at by the Apple "genius" who judged me when I inquired about a new charger! It still works and serves my purposes! Don't hate. My investment was a sound one. And when the device screen was damaged at school, I was reimbursed by my administration. Most teachers would be on their own. My administration also understands that the investment of time, energy, and money is the name of the game. Go to, and stay in places that honor your investment. One should not expect reimbursement, but we should take advantage of it when we have those resources.

Lebron James invests 1.5 million dollars into his body! And hasn't it paid off! Four NBA Championship rings are nothing to ignore! We need to be like Lebron. Now, I know our incomes are different! But the mindset is the same. I shiver when I hear the old sentiment that Teachers are broke. I am the first to admit that we are not paid our worth. We need to be united as teachers so across the country we have legislators that fight for our just compensation. Whatever our salary we need to use that money to reinvest in our practice, be the LeBron James of Teaching!

## Remote Teaching Expenses

Remote teaching has brought new financial burdens on teachers. Teaching (well) online can be expensive! Since remote learning began, I have purchased subscriptions to Zoom accounts upgraded software, joined organizations, obtained certifications, have taken trainings, purchased multiple mics, headphones, lighting equipment, green screens, keyboards, mice, computer chairs, water bottles, screen cleaner, extra chargers, power packs, and extension cords. My traveling teacher box used to contain things like pens and pencils. Now, I have chargers and chords for every device that beeps. The first headset I purchased only worked for certain situations, having a backup mic proved essential. The first mic for in-person teaching I used was a hand-held device and I soon learned that it dropped easily, and I needed something with Bluetooth capabilities. That launched into a new episode of trial and error. A green screen is wonderful, but scheppling it back and forth may mean you actually need two! And things break! They need replacing! Hybrid teaching is trial and error. Dynamic teaching is trial and error. You will invest money in getting this right. Other unexpected expenses arise also!

I have also stopped taking public transportation, and borrowed a car from a friend, and invested gas and maintenance into the vehicle, including parking passes/tickets! I have paid for multiple COVID tests and buckets upon buckets of sanitizer, bleach, and Clorox. My school purchased cleaning cloths for the laptops students use in school (as those are not provided). The school below us purchased individual desk shields for teacher desks. Teachers who are also parents have to invest in activities to keep their kids active while they work. They have also had to shell out cash for unpredictable child care situations when schools randomly close and open. It is a whirlwind and financial burden they were not expecting and often could not plan for.

## PPE (Personal Protective Equipment)

I was disgusted when I heard that in Arizona teachers would be required to supply their own PPE (Personal Protective Equipment). But, I realize I am spoiled! Our Union bargained for and got PPE supplied for all teachers (and students) on a monthly basis. But do we still buy our own PPE - yes! Some schools have invested in three or four-sided shields for each student's desk! Some of us go into the building with gloves and shields - some personalized and some disposable and the mix of both.

Teachers do not have much say if we are in the building or not. You either qualify to stay remote, or you do not. So despite my comfort level, school reopening is something I cannot control. What I *can* control is what I invest my money into to soothe my anxiety and up my preparedness. I can control the style and look of the mask/shields/gloves I wear. My PPE is truly personal, my face shield is personalized with the gold and silver puffy painted star that I painted on everything! My masks glitter and match the rhinestones on my shoes. The other sets match the brand on my t-shirts. One mask proudly tells the world I am an Extreme Teacher! My PPE is a fashion statement!

Wearing glasses makes PPE harder to work with! One day during in-person instruction, it was raining. I had on my mask, glasses, and face shield. Teachers now have to travel downstairs to pick up our students (like elementary school) so along with the workout, my face shield and glasses are constantly being fogged up! The trial and error of figuring out which masks you can breathe in and which mask/shield combo will agree with your glasses is a trip! On a daily basis, some of us were deciding if we needed to prioritize our seeing or breathing! It often depended on the moment which one was more important! I have purchased home thermometers to help monitor my health so I did not cause my school to shut down. I bring my own bottles of cleaning spray and also use the school-provided materials. I speak about and let my students see the cleaning taking place! It eases both of our fears and ensures we are all in the same place. Being real about our investment helps students take safety precautions more seriously also. I remind them to use the wall-mounted hand sanitizer supply, or the ones they brought with them. I invite them to place their sanitizer on their desks and give them wipes to clean their stations. We monitor how materials are distributed. I asked about students' level of comfortability before I handed out a handout or allowed them to engage in using a physical map. I also tracked student engagement to see who was comfortable and who was not. I have used laminated desk maps in the class, and students hear me say *"They have been sanitized"*, and see the careful way in which I distribute said maps. I gave them time to explore then collect the desk maps early so they can see me spray each one off before I leave the room. A wise woman once told me, *"Students are great observers but poor interpreters"*. You may never know a student is uncomfortable or offended by your actions until it comes up later! So being real about your personal investment in keeping the space and each other safe is a strong and needed message for our students. Some students are deathly afraid to re-enter the building. But when they see my microphone set, which allows them to hear me, and they see their teachers wearing two masks or a face shield, when they see us spraying down materials, when they see the custodian in his N-95 mask making rounds with the electromagnetic sprayer, it should bring comfort that we are keeping them in mind. Students should know specifically how their schools are *for* and *protect* them.

## Community Groups

One of the graduate-level requirements at the university I instruct at is to join a professional organization. Universities understand the need for teachers to invest in communities. Teachers need each other. One of the tasks is to identify the organizations that are truly supporting teachers and offering them legitimate services to fuel their practices. And like so many other services, you get what you pay for! It is an investment to become part of a subscription service for teachers. Other professionals have organizations that cater to them and their needs. It is an element of privilege to belong to organizations that feedback into their body of supporters. NYC has the largest teacher Union in the country as it serves the greatest number of teachers. Paying union dues ensures I have continued access to the protection, education, community, and resources they have to offer me. These services include counseling, student loan consultations, access to lawyers, meditators and lobbyists, tech support and healthcare protection, classes, transportation support, and so much UFT Swag!

The Community of Educators I have found since the pandemic is called Extreme Teachers and was founded by the #1 Motivational Speaker in the world - the Hip Hop Preacher Dr. Eric Thomas. Through the pandemic, Eric Thomas and his International Director of Education VaLarie Humphrey have created a cultural and educational epicenter. They offer free PDs (Professional Development) and paid certification opportunities along with their annual conference. Joining and helping build this community saved me and a litany of other teachers at the start of this pandemic. The New Teacher Project (TNTP) which is a non-profit organization that created and funded the Teaching Fellows program conducted PDs on how to combat the remedial teaching that may result from this pandemic. The Thriving Teacher Project is a dynamic organization that supports the socioemotional needs of teachers. Facing History & Ourselves is a curriculum-based organization that offers PDs and teacher based Professional Learning Communities (PLC) or small groups that meet and discuss the application of a said project, curriculum set, or theory. Do not forsake the gathering of the brethren - or sistren! I know that we can complain of being too busy, but God granted us each 24 hours in a day, and you find time for what is important. Collaboration is crucial to any teacher's success. Collaboration is crucial to any student's success. Collaboration is crucial to the world's growth and success.

## Invest in Them

As previously mentioned, every teacher reaches into their pocket on behalf of their students. Teachers have gotten creative in how they approach reaching out to their students. Snail mail has made a comeback! Those materials that are gathered, the personalization, the postage, the travel, the fees - it all adds up. Not to mention the sweat equity and other opportunity costs associated with sending packages to classes of 10-30 students. Time is an investment. How much extra time are you spending to support your students during a pandemic? I bet it was more time than before. The socioemotional needs of our students have expanded. I have had more private conversations and wake-up calls than ever before. Families need support and we reach out. Admin are holding virtual town halls, counselors are performing individual and group sessions, teachers are doing various forms of check-ins, all of which take time. I am cognizant about which students are receiving strategic intervention in the terms of time or money investment. We buy snacks and food as a form of investment. When I first started teaching, I instituted a Chai Chart as a form of positive behavioral support. Each day the students would need to follow a behavior model called *SWAG*. *S- Sit up, W- Wait silently to speak, A- Ask and Answer Questions, G- Give 100%, 100% of the time*! If each child was able to get a check on their SWAG chart, we could fill in a bar on the Chai Chart. At first, 5 consistent positive behavior days resulted in the prize - chai! When I studied abroad in Kenya, I learned how to make this delicious tea drink. So as I brewed this "coffee for kids" drink, I was teaching my students about African culture and the results of hard work. I was investing time and energy into their growth as human beings. In the same way, dynamic teaching involves finding incentives and investments for them. Class Dojo was another app that I used previously to support a PBIS (Positive Behavioral Interventions and Support) Model. The app allows students to create and customize a monster avatar with their name assigned to it. There are pre-set and customizable behaviors that students can get awarded points for. I modify the behaviors to represent the letters of SWAG and any other skills for the day that are being measured. Every time a student is awarded a point there is a delightful *ding* that fills the entire space with joy! The dopamine hit is just what we need! The services I have used here are free, but the time it takes to set this up is not.

Students need supplies. And as someone who has co-taught a science class, I know how many materials can be involved in a single lesson. Hybrid learning has put a new strain on science teachers and labs. What were once group projects became individual labs. Materials that could be shared, must now be sanitized and individualized. If there were seven groups, one needed seven graduated cylinders. Yet, in pods of 12-14 kids, we need 12-14 graduated cylinders! That is just one component of the lab - we use microscopes, rope, tape, beads, Petri dishes, beakers, stopwatches, syringes, goggles, scales, raw materials, dry materials, and wet materials. The *teacher* now has to be everyone's lab partner! And if your school's budget is not in a place to provide, teachers invest the financial equity by buying products themselves or investing in online curriculum and videos that provide visual aids to help close the gap. Or we invest emotional and time equity to be creative as we search for new solutions, where maybe half of the class is performing a lab, and the other class is focusing on the writing standards necessary for a science and technical language based course. Our students often do not see the labor of love we put in. Especially now when they cannot see the gigantic carts of science and art supplies that need to be schlepped across the school. They do not see piles of maps and whiteboard trays that need to be sanitized after every period. They do not see the receipts for online platforms and tickets to conferences and PDs. We can share this with them without complaining about our circumstances. But if we share how we invest in them, it can inspire them to invest in themselves.

## GEMs

- ❖ "Invest in You & Them" means that we must spend money and time on ourselves before we are able to lead others.

- ❖ Be the Lebron James of teaching. Do not let others belittle you for spending your own money on your craft. It will pay dividends. Look for the return on your investment in student outcomes.

- ❖ New expenses arise from tech needs, commuting changes, childcare expenses, and more.

- ❖ Investing money into communities can help regulate the above expenses and needs.

- ❖ After you have invested in you, investing in them (our students) is a more healthy and sustainable endeavor.

# CHAPTER 9

# T - Tenacity

The struggle is real. While I come as an ambassador of hope, I also come as a partner in pain. The hybrid teaching situation has turned teacher lions into teacher kittens. It has prompted early retirement, early sabbaticals, early balding, early menopause, and increased teacher turnover. Current events hit differently in isolation. Teachers have had to become mighty warriors in order to face these times. The difference is, they have had to use weapons they have never wielded before. Evolve or die. But that does not mean that it does not hurt.

**The "T" in "Shine Brite" stands for Tenacity.**

**<u>Face Current Events</u>**

We had a summer of vivid and memorialized police-sanctioned violence committed on black bodies accompanied by videos and images that have burned into memory. We saw black bodies murdered in real time. We are witnessing Asian Americans and Pacific Islanders defending their lives against racist accusations and shootings rooted in a new level of intellectual ignorance fueled by social media, misinformation, and yellow journalism. This is America. We see cycles of hatred persist.

While the virus spread we saw hospitals filled and statistical evidence telling us our time was coming. We have had our cities shut down completely. Curfew and lockdowns. Promises were made and broken. Wartime and great depression scenarios we had only read about or heard from grandparents became our reality.

### *Say Something - They're Giving Up on You*

I sang a cover of this song during one of my "Motivation 4 Teachers Amid COVID" videos when I charged Teachers to speak about police brutality. Some educators thought it was okay to keep quiet when the world was raging. It did not take me long to realize I had a message to send to my fellow teachers: use your voice and position to speak out against hatred, violence, discrimination, bias, and injustice. I know as a black child growing up attending white institutions how loud silence can be. My admin allowed me to say this to our staff, and encourage them to speak.

My Principal has, on more than one occasion, sent out emails to the entire school community affirming our stance about human rights and equality for multiple subgroups of people. I applaud that, and when I do not know what to say I simply re-read the email to the class. When "45" was elected, we were given an article about what to say. So through tears with a broken voice, I read to my Hispanic students that we would do everything in our democratic power to protect them. I read to my female students that their bodies are sacred and we would protect them too. My male co-teachers read and modeled what true integrity and manhood should look like.

It is the responsibility of every single educator in America to create and shape the citizens of America. If America is racist, the teachers are racist. If America is sexist, the teachers are sexist. If America is xenophobic, the teachers are xenophobic. If America is ignorant, the teachers are ignorant.

We cannot allow hatred, violence, discrimination, bias, and injustice to persist in our classrooms. We must use our voice and position to reduce the possibility of them surviving in our streets and homes. I was the first Black woman who was not a nanny some of my students had ever seen. I may be the first Black woman with multiple graduate degrees they have ever seen, though statistically, that does not compute. According to the American Association of University Women, "Black women earn 64.1% of bachelor's degrees, 71.5% of master's degrees, and 65.9% of doctoral, medical, and dental degrees." Speaking of Tenacity, Black women are "the most Educated group in the US". Yet less than 5.2% of us are professors (do not even ask about tenure tracks)!

We cannot shy away from the issues facing our nation. When an unjust action decimates the community around your school, give your students space to discuss it. When the nation erupts with anti-AAPI violence, stand up and tell your students it is wrong. Even when you feel you do not have the right words, it does not excuse you from speaking. There are a plethora of other educated individuals who are writing about and speaking on these topics. Use their voice if you cannot find your own.

You have the right as an educator to teach children to be critical thinkers, and you have a responsibility to be a just person. Every teacher should be able to say, "Black Lives Matter" and keep it pushing. Someone in the class may pipe up "Blue Lives Matter too!" This is true! It is important to acknowledge all perspectives, but remind students that the latter was never up for debate. You should never have an open argument with a student. Get support if you suspect a conversation could become contentious. Be honest about your limitations. But you must stand up against hate and hate-based violence. You need to be able to say hate against the LGBTQ+ community is wrong. You do not need to be able to teach about the acronym to know that killing someone and spouting hate speech is wrong. You need to acknowledge the disrespect (and almost erasure) of indigenous people in our nation. Muslim students should be protected from the hate-based violence and fear that spread after 9/11. Hispanic students should be protected from the fear-mongering leading to questionable policies that spread when "45" began his campaign trail. Female students should be protected from acts of sexual harassment that exist in male-dominated spaces. *Freedom of speech in America does not equate to the Freedom to hate in our school systems.* Our country lets you hate in the streets, but our schools should be sacred spaces. It is not your job to say everything - but it *is* your job to say something.

## **Death**

The amount of death and loss is staggering. We can barely process our emotions as we strive to ensure students are okay. Yet, how do we do this when our very systems of connection are cut off at the root? Some of us literally went from full classrooms one day to no classroom or student interaction for almost two weeks! Some of us were just making headway then lost contact with kids due to limited Wi-Fi and/or their inability to self-motivate. Relationships were shattered by death, sickness, and the true colors of people that come out during quarantine. *"I see your true colors shining through - and I don't like you"* was often the case. And yet, our primary profession and job expectations did not change. As professional educators, we are still expected to get through the minutiae and trauma of life. How? How do we deal with all the death?

First, we must face it. Do not for one moment act like this experience hasn't completely rocked your teaching world. Even if you are a first-year teacher and were "born into this", your educational experience could in no way prepare you to face this. So that fancy teacher training they gave you in grad school, did not give you everything I am giving you in this book. My graduate school education did include a component called "digital competencies" that required students to produce online content. But this small production was nothing compared to what teachers were tasked to do this year.

Virtual and hybrid teaching was not created to be sustained. Yet, we have to maintain. Tenacity means teaching like this may be the last lesson we ever teach because it very well could be. The next day you could be gone. The next day a child could be gone. And I mean for good. We must face our mortality in new ways. My health is not just connected to *my* mortality. This pandemic requires me to be health conscious for those around me, as well as for myself.

## **Respond to the Seasons**

Dynamic teachers know that the seasons and months are not created equal. In Arizona, the Christmas break lasts for three weeks in December making it a moot teaching month. In New York City, state and religious holidays make the start of school and the fall interesting to track! We need to be attuned to how students respond to the seasons of school and the seasons prior to the break. We must respond to the emotional needs that Valentine's Day or Thanksgiving might trigger for lonely students. We sometimes observe kids acting differently due to the weather changes or the house they are presently staying at. Some may be living in or have had to return to living in shelters or foster care. We must respond to their current living situation as we address the current events of our nation and cities.

For instance, if I know a child lost a parent, why on earth would I hound them for homework? If I can see a child who was previously engaged pull back, why on earth would I not inquire whether or not some kind of life change has happened? It is not surprising that the students who have been struggling the most are the "life-of-the-party" social butterflies. I have seen kids who were social savants crippled by remote social interaction, or worse, glitching software. Yet, I have also seen wallflowers blossom in the chat. As teachers, we must support the first type of student, while praising and acknowledging the ones who are making it look easy. We work to bridge the gap and respond when things shift. We push those who are excelling to use their access to technology in new and dynamic ways. We create alternate tasks and schedules for those who are struggling to survive. We have extra meetings with parents and guardians. We perform wake-up calls and listening conferences. We create check-ins using applications like *Remind* or *Class Dojo*. We find ways to give students credit for showing up and create distance learning rubrics that are responsive to our community's needs.

Some schools do not require students to turn their cameras on in order to be responsive to each family's situation. My school community requires it, but also makes access to getting devices very accessible. Educators cannot require something of students they have not provided tools for. This is crippling and demoralizing. For if I give you a requirement without giving you the tools to fulfill it, I have crippled you.

Believe it or not, students are still sharing their pain, but not always in healthy ways. Social Media has allowed students to not just reach out and support each other, but also share in and create more trauma. Students scribble goodbye messages and turn group chats into crisis intervention teams. They document self-harm and share it privately and publicly. They re-trigger each other with jokes and mean-spirited comments. New apps make it easier to express your joy and creativity but can also bring your darkest demons to light. Teachers need to know this. We need to respond when we see students in crisis. Repeatedly, we need to remind them that we and other resources exist. I am not suggesting we turn into counselors for all of our students. Love alone does not equip teachers to counsel 300+ students each week! But I always have our school counselor on speed dial. She responds to my texts in a timely way and I have spent more than one afternoon calling hotlines and filing reports for students and families who need extra care.

We are using the emergency systems effectively. Not every school has its appointed psychologist, guidance counselor, therapist, and social worker in place. But use what you have and demand what you need. You know the people in our community who have the heart and gifts to serve without the degrees and titles. Does your school secretary have the gift of connection? Do you know the lunch lady who has a special connection with the student everyone worries is "lost"? Do you know the para has a side business and happens to live in the same neighborhood as the kids who need him the most? Do you know your principal is a baller and stays after games to help kids with fundamentals? Do you know the Spanish teacher may be the right person to talk to Spanish-speaking parents about HS and College options since she has raised and supported her own children through grad school? Do you know the art teacher may be the best person to support students who return to school from a psychiatric episode? Do you know the parent coordinator is willing to take public transport to reach ANY of your students? Do you know students are willing to step up and lead each other over troubled waters? Use what is in your hand. The dozens of talented and supportive hands of the school building, even if we are connecting via Wi-Fi. We are still connecting.

## **Mourn**

If you have not taken a moment to mourn, let it out. It is okay to hurt, and as humans, we *should* hurt. Since we experience cycles and new waves of trauma, it is appropriate to create cycles and new waves of healing. The Thriving Teacher Project was birthed from the need for Teachers to have a space to heal, transform, and continue to fight. I first met Mia Tan (the young, beautiful, brilliant, talented, and brave CEO) near the start of the pandemic when she saw my video *Prayer for Anxious Teachers*. I have since become a disciple of the work she is doing. She brings educational trauma-informed gurus to the virtual spaces we need them most. It helps me mourn and move on when another incident rocks us.

There are kids who lost an educational year, that *should* hurt you teacher. You love your students, and I know you worked hard to make this not so, but your emails fell on deaf ears, your postcards and care packages came back undeliverable, your texts were left unread, your phone/zoom calls were denied or never answered. You intended to get the child a device, and someone (maybe even you) dropped the ball. You may have missed an email when someone *did* try to reach out, but time passed, and you never could re-engage them. Or the school building opened a little too late and that child tried to, or worse completed the act of committing suicide. We literally lost some of our babies. And that *should* hurt you teacher. We figuratively lost some of our babies. And that *should* hurt you teacher. Students we taught last year are now with teachers who have never seen their faces and cannot make that same connection. We do not have the resources to tell them what we know. We do not have enough resources to track their progress from afar. And even if we did, some students just prefer to be alone with their grief. Can we blame them? Our students have faced the death of grandparents,

parents, siblings, peers, aunts, uncles, cousins, families, marriages, homes, schools, dozens of friendships, free time, freedom, innocence, work time, support, sports, teammates, identity.

And so have we.

Teachers have died. Many school personnel have died. The United Federation of Teachers (UFT) created a dedication page with running names and pictures of the school staff that were lost to COVID-19. Some of us are re-entering the buildings knowing our friends are never coming back. We did not properly get to say goodbye when schools closed, and now we did not properly get to say goodbye when they passed away. A Zoom funeral is not a replacement for an in-person homegoing ceremony. And if a person's extended family is not aware of our connection, we may not have been told of funeral services. Due to the stigma associated with this virus, some of us could not support like we wanted to since the family wanted or needed privacy. That creates holes in the healing journey and gaps that can lead to stunting intellectual growth. How can I begin to use Nearpod when I am not sure if my teacher best friend is returning to the building or not? Or if their parents are still alive? So much is unknown causing us to fret and fear. The what-ifs are continuous and the pain is palpable. People I saw 180 days a year for the last eight years, I have now not seen in over 365 days. I would give ANYTHING to once again be in the auditorium with everyone that was in my school building in Spring 2020 again. But that literally will never ever happen. And it hurts.

*Pause. That hit hard, and I need to cry.*

## Ugly Cry & Wailing Women

Most of us know the term "ugly cry" by now. 2020 has given us plenty of reasons to and examples of what an ugly cry looks like. Mouth agape, all twisted up, eyes swollen and contorted, snot and slobber over everything, shoulders heaving, and body weak.

This is not time to be cute. We have embraced the ugly cry because there comes a time in everyone's life where it is warranted. Everyone may not do it in public, but I do not believe anyone is exempt from it at least once in their lifetime. As a Christian and Black Baptist, I am well-versed in the nature of homegoing services (aka funerals). My mother is an anointed singer and has been asked on multiple occasions to sing at the homegoing services of fellow saints. I have attended these services and seen amazing results of her songs infused with God's comfort on the people in the audience. Her songs and her ability to wail and cry with her voice, allow the family to unleash their emotions. Jeremiah 9:17-22 NIV version says

> "This is what the Lord Almighty says: 'Consider now! Call for the wailing women to come; send for the most skillful of them. Let them come quickly and wail over us till our eyes overflow with tears and water streams from our eyelids... Teach your daughters how to wail; teach one another a lament. Death has climbed in through our windows and has entered our fortresses; it has cut off the children from the streets and the young men from the public squares... The dead bodies of men will lie like refuse on the open field, like cut grain behind the reaper. with no one to gather them."

WHOO! Sound familiar? This is a time where we need "wailing women" to help deal with the trauma of these times.

My grandmother, Diamond Hudson, taught her daughter, Naomi Skinner, how to wail. Naomi Skinner, my mother, taught her daughter, Diamond Emelda *(translation of Emerald)*, how to wail. We may not have seen this coming. But we can lean on the wisdom of our ancestors to walk through it and overcome it. Let this book and my songs help you let it out. And deal with whatever is lying in wait for you to conquer.

*I am a skilled Wailing Woman.*
*I am the Teacher's Wailing Woman.*

## GEMs

- ❖ Having "Tenacity" means dealing with the issues we face as teachers as well as the issues our country and communities face.

- ❖ The Struggle is Real - Don't pretend it's not.

- ❖ Death has happened literally and figuratively. Use the village as a healing source.

- ❖ How have you mourned? How are you mourning? How will you mourn in the future?

- ❖ I am the Teacher's Wailing Woman Wailing Woman

# CHAPTER 10

# E - Execute

*Go to Work.* I mean that literally and, if possible, physically. Virtual learning is not a vacation. There is a litany of critics who presume that our time spent out of the building is "free time" for us teachers. Unfortunately, there is also a subset of our colleagues who have taken advantage of working from home. There are standards our profession demands. I did not say job, I said profession. We are professionals. I love my Union's slogan, *A Union of Professionals* since critics are constantly trying to undermine our work. We are not babysitters; we are caretakers of children. We are not "workhorses", but our career does require homework. We are not cogs in a machine but are an essential voice in dismantling systems that say we are. We cannot change the fabric of America if we refuse to sit at the loom.

### The "E" in "Shine Brite" stands for "Execute".

### Execute

*"Execution is Worshipped!"* says the Hip Hop Preacher Dr. Eric Thomas. I vibe with this quote and reality. One of the reasons I chose to join this mighty profession is that I knew that teachers made a difference

on the daily. We do not wrestle with theories then expect answers in the distant future. Our theories are tested out in real-time, our sprouts bloom before our eyes. Now- that *does not* mean we see kids make grade level jumps overnight, but that *does* mean every day we are executing at our highest level which inevitably leads to student growth. Every day when my head hits the pillow I can say with sincerity, *Well done, Diamond.* Even on the days I mess up, I did not mess up every kid! I know from personal experience how bad it hurts to fail. I know how it feels to teach a lesson incorrectly. The late, great, educator Rita Pearson tells her TedTalk story about teaching a lesson all wrong. The students knew and when she apologized (teacher, take the hint!) they replied, *"You were just so excited, we just let you go"!* She may have taught that content lesson wrong, but the lesson about education being exciting was the real meat and potatoes of her story! My students know how seriously I take this profession, education, and their lives. *Do Yours?*

I have said time and time again to my students that they need to "Fight for their Lives". Teacher, are you doing the same? Are you fighting to preserve your sanity, safety, and well-being during this time? There are teacher support groups. Are you going? If you are not tapping into your self-care practices, how are you modeling this for them?

There are free workshops to educate using e-learning. Are you attending? There are free virtual courses on YouTube like *Tech Savvy Teacher* on my page. Are you re-watching material until you learn it? Practice what you preach! If you are not making the most of virtual learning, why should your students?

And if you are refusing to come back into the buildings, why should they? I know full well that some teachers have qualified for and obtained medical accommodations from the states they work for to work remotely due to a pre-existing medical condition. But let us be real. When you see a school with 100% of its teachers remote, it is not rampant asthma or obesity, it is a collective decision to not return to the building. The Union, our custodians, our district representatives, our legislators, our principals, our school safety officers, our resource officers, our *everythings*, have worked to keep the building safe and write legislation that keeps us safe. We know there have been bad decisions made, but will you live there or live beyond? You must consider what is best for your students and how you can work to meet them in their needs. You know it is best for them to be in the building. So do not get confused or frustrated about things you do *not* know. You do not know if an infection will shut down your school. But you do know they need people in the building. You do not know if the vaccination will fully protect you. But you do know that every day certain students spend out of the classroom is a lost instructional time. Every lost instructional period is loss of life! You create Academic Growth or you create Academic Death! The power of life and death is in your hands teacher!

If you do not know how powerful you are, I am here to tell you. You are the sustainer of their education. You are the pillar of that school building. You are the end-all and be-all when it comes to their academic life. You are the bridge between students graduating and sleeping under those same bridges. You are the ones who can bring kids out of their social dilemmas and depression. You are the ones who keep schools open virtually and during hybrid learning. You are the ones connecting with kids with cameras on or off. You are the ones who transition on the spot when schools are suddenly closed. You are the ones students talk to when they cannot reach their advisor. You are the ones who show up daily so they know that school is still in session. *Do not model giving up, model going through!* Model that grit and growth mindset we made all those posters about! This is when the Master Teachers rise up! This is when we split the novices from the dynamic Highly Effective educators.

*Execute*

*Execute*

*Execute*

*In the midst of Adversity, Execute*

*- Dr. Eric Thomas*

I heard ET say it, and I bought the T-shirt to help me manifest it. When I started teaching, I vowed to be such a great special educator that students wished they had disabilities to be in my class. And I made it happen.

When remote teaching started I vowed to be the beast at virtual teaching just like I was for in-person teaching. I refused to let this beat me. And I made it happen. Am I an expert at every virtual learning platform? Nope! But I know how to use digital competencies to enhance my online lessons and I learn quickly enough to adapt. I have students who I have only met virtually, and they love me to life! I started teaching other teachers how to provide service and thrive during the pandemic on a daily basis. The culmination of that work is manifested in your reading of this text.

When I was in High School, another highly motivated peer and I bemoaned how all the world's big issues had been solved. I desired a purpose and a problem to solve. I asked for my Civil Rights movement and I got it. Follow me into Zion. Follow me into the school systems we must create. Do not waste time on Facebook, Twitter, and other social media platforms complaining about our lot, we are teachers! We are a part of a privileged profession in America. And if your state does not see that, be such a professional that it gives cause for parents and administrators to rise up and demand you get the respect you deserve. But we will not get it by being mediocre and refusing to return to the building.

## Should I leave my school?

You may have to leave your school and its toxic environment. But do not for one moment think that leaving your school for another will instantly solve your problems. You are already a new teacher to hybrid learning but you have a year under your belt with this school. Starting at a new school will mean that you are a new teacher again, new to whatever teaching model they have. You will have new admin and new colleagues to learn. Do not fall into the trap that the Wi-Fi is always better in the other building. Maybe it is not! The best Wi-Fi in the world and the most effective curriculums will never replace the positive collegial relationships that are formed and cultivated amongst the people in your school. If you have established strong trusting relationships with your fellow teachers, it is worth sticking around for another year. Even on my best days as a first-year teacher, I did not (and could not) develop relationships overnight.

If you have found an ally in an administrator and they have supported you beyond what is expected, it is worth sticking around another year. If you have bonded with students whom you know would have floundered without you, it is worth sticking around another year.

If not you, then who? If you know the struggle is real, aren't you more equipped than the next joker who would come behind you? Like Drake said, "I started from the bottom now we're here!" If you leave your school you need to be prepared to do the same! So consider yourself to be at an advantage no matter where you are in the game. You are in the game! And it is up to us to stay in the game.

## Administration

Not all administrators are created equal. I have seen my Vice Principal get jostled in the hallway while on her way to cover a teacher's class. So how can I complain when it happens to me? I know principals who drive kids back and forth from the building or events during late hours. So how can I complain when a project keeps me in the building late? I have seen my principal hold himself accountable in the middle of a hallway after a disciplinary incident and ask the teachers around, *Did I do the right thing?* So why would I not stop to question myself and my actions when they ask me to?

I know administrators who come early and stay late as a lifestyle. I know administrators who spend their own money on teacher's expenses just like we spend our own money on our students. I know administrators who turn the other cheek when they know we are dead wrong. I know administrators who have lost their lives to the pandemic and left holes in their school buildings because their leadership was so effective. I know administrators who have worked in the building despite it being closed or not. They model what they want from their teachers and support them along the way.

I am aware there are tyrants, but they get no space here in this book. I would not have been able to write this book if I was well versed with tyrannical leadership. But when a Teaching Fellow or one of my college students comes to me with the ails of working in such an environment I ponder, *Well they can't be in your classroom all the time, can they?* And now, even virtually, they still are not going to watch every bit of video footage made available to them. Work through the systems of oppression - do not succumb to them!

Maybe your school requires cameras on, but you know a collection of your class will not go for it. Demonstrate how you can get engagement despite it, rather than preparing an excuse for why cameras are off during your observation. If you have to save face during an observation and say something like, *"Hi Josh! I would love to see your face today!"* to demonstrate you tried.

Maybe your school experienced a spike in retirements or pregnancy during the pandemic and now the building is even less staffed than before. You know your health and are smart enough to do the research about things that concern you. Come back into the building. Every day, we used to be there with gross children who did not know how to properly blow their noses! In many ways, it is safer now than it was back then! As the legislation continues to relax, the pressure to return will be greater or required. Prepare your mindset, to prepare for the legislation.

## **Lesson Planning**

There is no formal way to prepare lesson plans that are 100% effective. My advice is to plan them anyway! "*Those who fail to plan plan to fail*", Granny always said. In the same way, do not be caught off guard. The Shine Brite Lesson Plan Template I provide here is an adapted format that is a combination of past templates and ones that integrate new systems of education research, and differentiation based on student need. One thing that has remained consistent is double planning. You need to clearly know what you are doing throughout the lesson and what each set of students is also doing. Before hybrid teaching, the right column was "what students were doing", now you potentially need to prepare for "both sets" of in-person and remote students. This means we must create in-person learning and remote learning simultaneously. We should get paid twice as much! Until that happens, demonstrate the *need* for that to happen! Show your prowest as an educator with every keyboard stroke and double plan that matches the Danielson rubric so that you (and everyone else) know how you execute for the betterment of your students. We are working with children, there is no margin for error! We have to execute now, and every day, despite the possibility of shutdowns - we look toward the future. And when the schools randomly shut down midweek, we will execute anyway. One of the hardest times to execute (besides when loved ones were dying) was when Spring Break was canceled in 2020. I leaned on Nico and Vinz to create the cover of this song. Even if you do not have the same privileges mentioned below, we still have way much more to rejoice about, than complain about.

*"I look in the mirror and I ask myself- self- self who I see.*
*Who I'm becoming and If I will stand up for My ( I I I ) beliefs. Mulgrew*
*told us that we are essential - we're in an Emergency! And my teacher and I*
*am so grateful that moneys not taken from me.*
*Ohh! I was teaching and learning and trying to find a home! (Ohh) With*
*this pandemic raging I'm grateful I'm left behind! Yea! I know what I've got!*
*Yea! I know what we've got. We've got pensions, good jobs and healthcare so*
*I won't waste my time saying things are not fair! Yeah! I know what we've*
*got - Yeah! I know what we've got.*
*We've got pensions, good work and healthcare so I won't waste my time*
*saying things are not fair!"*

The time we spend complaining about the new platforms could be used to learn to execute with them. The time we spend trolling social media and blasting each other and our leaders could be spent creating content that engages our students in real ways. There is so much out there to tear us down, and you purchased this book to be built up!

*Shine Teacher, Shine on, and Shine Brite!*
*Don't you dare stop now!*
*You are Dynamic!*
*You are a Diamond!*
*Lives depend on YOU!*
*Execute*
*Execute*

*Execute*

*In and Out of Pandemics, Execute!*

## GEMs

- ❖ "Execute" means Go to Work. Kids need us in the building.

- ❖ If you cannot go into the building, execute as an *exceptional* remote educator.

- ❖ Execution is Worshipped.

- ❖ Administrators are heroes too! Execute despite the tyrants.

- ❖ Continue the *"Shine Brite"* journey online with the Facebook group & email list!

- ❖ Invite me to your school for small and large group PDs to put these principles into action.

- ❖ You have 2020 vision - now use it!

### *FEAR NOT AND SHINE BRITE!*

# *About The Author*

Diamond Emerald is a veteran educator who facilitates professional development for new teachers so they can become career educators and transform their lives and those of their students. She is the retention guru and helps new teachers deliver exceptional instruction by implementing the strategies they are working to master. She's earned undergraduate degrees from Washington University in St. Louis, and Master's Degrees from NYU & Hunter College. She was an NYC Teacher Fellow and began teaching teachers after just two years! She is also an adjunct at Hunter College teaching teachers how to pass the Edtpa Teacher Certification Exam. She also conducts Professional Development around NYC and speaks at National Teacher's Conferences. She has years of experience coaching New Teachers to their Excellence. As a Certified Extreme Teacher, she uses her knowledge of the DISC personality assessment to encourage, motivate and coach teachers to go from good to phenomenal! She loves to eat gummies, and to sing, act, dance, and write.

- *"Fear Not & Shine Brite"!*

*For booking contact:*
*diamond@diamondemerald.com*

Social Media handles
Twitter @1DiamondEmerald
Instagram @diamondemerald11
TikTok @diamondemerald11
Youtube Diamond Emerald
youtube.com/c/diamondemerald

www.ingramcontent.com/pod-product-compliance
Lightning Source LLC
Chambersburg PA
CBHW071137280326
41935CB00010B/1261